Praise for *Journal of the Dead*

"Wholly absorbing. . . . Tells the story of Coughlin and Kodikian with quiet authority, lending unexpected dignity to the whole affair." —*New York Times Book Review*

"One hell of a fascinating ride." —*National Geographic Adventure*

"Five stars. As tough to put down as Jon Krakauer's *Into the Wild*." —*Maxim*

"This book is so addictive, I advise not cracking it until you have enough time to read it straight through. . . . Kersten has a keen, almost noirish, sense of suspense." —*Time Out* (New York)

"A taut, expertly researched true-crime narrative." —*Boston Herald*

"A gripping, readable tale." —*Austin American-Statesman*

"A fascinating case, a fascinating book." —Anderson Cooper, CNN

"Fascinating." —*Oregonian*

"A story that is inherently interesting, and one you can't read without wondering . . . what you would do in a similar situation." —*Rocky Mountain News*

"Deftly penned by Jason Kersten, a rising star in the journalism world. . . . Resounding [and] unforgettable." —*Denver Westword*

"One of those rare books that the reader will be compelled to read in a single sitting. . . . It's that good." —*Tulsa World*

"A brilliant new book . . . in the great nonfiction tradition of Jon Krakauer's *Into the Wild*." —*Advertising Age*

"Kersten's direct prose creates a very real scene. . . . The reader . . . can't help but feel for all involved in this perplexing and tragic scenario." —*Library Journal*

"A true American tragedy, beautifully written. *Journal of the Dead* is one of those books you'll always want on your shelf."
—Tony Hillerman, author of *The Sinister Pig*

"*Journal of the Dead* is more than a fine read and a riveting portrait of the American desert. It is the debut of a strong writer whose crystalline prose stands as an example of what writing should be."
—William Langewiesche, author of *American Ground*

"This is a story that interested me from the moment it was first reported. Jason Kersten has gone behind the headlines and uncovered the true story of what happened in Rattlesnake Canyon. It's a riveting story, a page-turner, a book that I couldn't put down."
—Lawrence Schiller, author of *Perfect Murder, Perfect Town*

"A provocative and deeply disturbing study of unexpected tragedy in the New Mexico desert when two friends lose their way. Harrowing and heart-wrenching, Kersten's penetrating and tautly written account of one friend's 'mercy killing' of his best friend continues to haunt long after the story is over: when, if ever, is such a killing justifiable?"

—Dick Lehr, coauthor of *Judgment Ridge* and *Black Mass*

"A brilliantly crafted exploration of a profoundly human mystery. Jason Kersten's portrait of these two young men, of the choices they make and—especially—of the unforgiving beauty of the desert itself leaves a searing impression. It will leave you wondering: could the desert really be so cruel that you would beg your best friend to take your life?"

—Victoria Bruce, author of *No Apparent Danger*

"A gripping adventure narrative with a touch of backcountry *CSI*. Ours is not to divine what really happened in that remote New Mexico canyon, but Kersten presents the evidence in lucid, logical, riveting fashion, letting the reader draw their own conclusions. A page-turner." —Martin Dugard, author of *Into Africa*

About the Author

JASON KERSTEN is a senior editor at *Maxim* magazine and holds a master's degree from Columbia University's Graduate School of Journalism. He lives in New York City.

JOURNAL
of the
DEAD

JOURNAL
of the
DEAD

———

A STORY OF FRIENDSHIP AND MURDER
IN THE NEW MEXICO DESERT

———

JASON
KERSTEN

Perennial

An Imprint of HarperCollins*Publishers*

A hardcover edition of this book was published in 2003 by
HarperCollins Publishers.

JOURNAL OF THE DEAD. Copyright © 2003 by Jason Kersten.
All rights reserved. Printed in the United States of America.
No part of this book may be used or reproduced in any manner
whatsoever without written permission except in the case
of brief quotations embodied in critical articles and reviews.
For information address HarperCollins Publishers Inc.,
10 East 53rd Street, New York, NY 10022.

HarperCollins books may be purchased for educational, business,
or sales promotional use. For information please write: Special
Markets Department, HarperCollins Publishers Inc.,
10 East 53rd Street, New York, NY 10022.

First Perennial edition published 2004.

Designed by Stephanie Huntwork

Map by David Cain

The Library of Congress has catalogued the hardcover edition as
follows:

Kersten, Jason.
Journal of the dead: a story of friendship and murder in the
New Mexico desert / Jason Kersten.—1st ed.
p. cm.
ISBN 0-06-018470-1
1. Homicide—New Mexico—Carlsbad Caverns National Park.
2. Murder—New Mexico—Carlsbad Caverns National Park.
3. Kodikian, Raffi. 4. Coughlin, David Andrew, d. 1999.
I. Title.

HV6533.N4K47 2003
364.15'23'0978942—dc21   2003040714

ISBN 0-06-095922-3 (pbk.)

04 05 06 07 08 ❖/RRD 10 9 8 7 6 5 4 3 2 1

For Judy

And he said to me, "Stand beside me and slay me; for anguish has seized me, and yet my life still lingers."

So I stood beside him, and slew him, because I was sure that he could not live after he had fallen; and I took the crown which was on his head and the armlet which was on his arm, and I have brought them here to my lord.

—SAMUEL 2:1

A good friend stabs you in the front.

—OSCAR WILDE

AUTHOR'S NOTE

Rattlesnake Canyon is a remote, mostly unheard-of rift in the New Mexican desert. Compared to monumental terrestrial clefts like the Grand and Bryce Canyons, it is just a crack—five miles long, seven hundred feet deep, and typically bone dry. But in the early hours of Sunday, August 8, 1999, it became a moral fracture as well.

Most of the people who heard Raffi Kodikian's story found themselves standing on one side or the other. Some believed that what happened there, though horrific, was an understandable act, committed out of compassion under incredible physical and mental duress. Others believed that nothing could justify such a decision, and that only the most careless, insensitive, or deranged human being would act as Kodikian had. And still more were convinced that the story Kodikian told was an ingenious lie, designed to hide the truth of an enraged murder.

It was that very ambiguity, along with an interest in the landscape, that drew me to write about the Rattlesnake Canyon case in the January 2000 issue of *Maxim* magazine. After that piece was published, a message board was created on *Maxim*'s website, and hundreds of young men logged on to comment and debate whether or not Kodikian should be given leniency. The only thing people could agree on was that his story was extraordinary and just plain bizarre. His knife had pierced more than his friend's heart. It had struck a collective nerve.

As I began writing this book, I felt great pressure to take a side myself. Like most people, I simply could not imagine doing what Kodikian did, to anyone, much less my best friend. And indeed history tells us that the choice he made—despite the hellacious circumstances—is by far the exception, not the rule. The easiest explanation for Kodikian's behavior has always been that he had motivations other than mercy, and there is certainly ample circumstantial fuel for that fire. But if that is true, then to me it makes his story even more extraordinary, because he appears to be quite a well-adjusted young man. Here was a guy who was raised in an upper-middle-class home by a loving family. He adored books and travel, studied journalism, fell in love during college, wrestled with jobs he didn't like while pursuing his writing, and had good friends with whom he enjoyed laughing and drinking beer. He could be me or fifty people I know. As far as which side of the canyon I stand on, I will claim the storyteller's privilege and say only that I'd pity anyone picked to be a juror on a case such as this one.

Re-creating what happened in Rattlesnake Canyon presented certain problems; the only living witness, Raffi Kodikian himself, chose not to be interviewed about the matter any further. That portion of this book is therefore based on his court testimony, the journal the friends kept, and physical evidence, along with law enforcement documents, my own interviews, and explorations of the terrain. I present it as fact, and leave it up to the reader to believe it or not.

For obvious reasons, I could not include all of the court testimony in the *State of New Mexico v. Raffi Kodikian*. For the purposes of narrative, I shortened both witness testimony and examination by the lawyers, focusing instead on those sections I believe constituted the crux of each argument. I did not, however, alter the chronology of testimony or the quotes used in any way.

Last, if you come across Raffi Kodikian, please leave him in peace. What each of us decides to believe about his motivations probably says more about how we prefer to see ourselves than it does about him. Raffi is, as they say, square with the house, and my intention in writing this book wasn't to make his life or the lives of the Coughlin family more difficult. It was to tell the story of a criminal case that was one in a million, and at the very least to make people more aware of the precautions they should take if they decide to explore the priceless treasures of America's deserts.

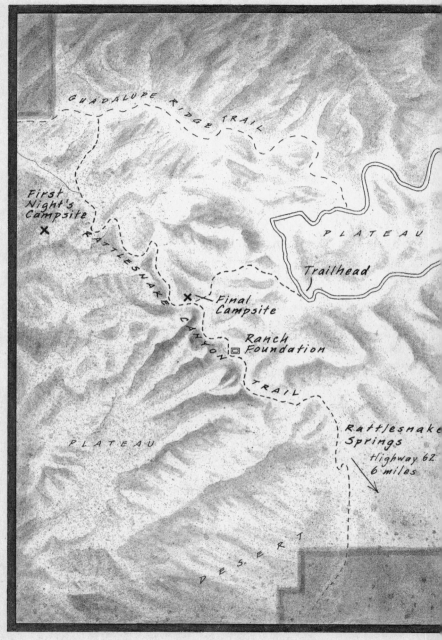

Rattlesnake Canyon, Carlsbad Caverns National Park, New Mexico.

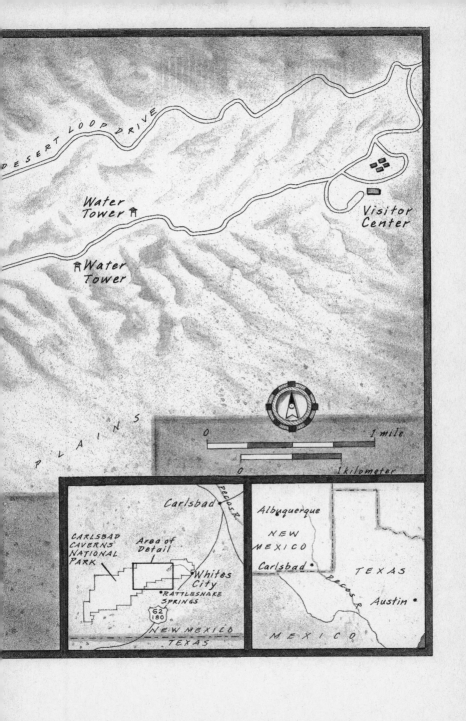

DESERT LOOP DRIVE

Water Tower

Water Tower

Visitor Center

PLAINS

0   1 mile

0   1 kilometer

Carlsbad

Pecos R.

CARLSBAD CAVERNS NATIONAL PARK

Area of Detail

Whites City

•RATTLESNAKE SPRINGS

62 180

NEW MEXICO

TEXAS

Albuquerque

NEW MEXICO

Carlsbad •

TEXAS

Pecos R.

Austin •

MEXICO

JOURNAL
of the
DEAD

PART ONE

1

There's an old story people still tell their children in New Mexico. It took place in 1598, when the Spanish founders of Santa Fe were forced to cross the hostile Chihuahuan Desert. Stretching from central Mexico to just south of Albuquerque, the Chihuahuan nearly wiped out the two hundred colonists by sapping away their water. They wandered through the cacti and tumbleweeds half mad for a week, and were spared an excruciating death only by a fortuitous rain. Afterward, they came to call the most brutal part of the desert *el Jornada del Muerto,* "the journey of the dead."

Lance Mattson didn't need to hear the old tales about the Spanish to know what the desert could do to people. As a twenty-eight-year-old ranger at Carlsbad Caverns National Park, which sits inside a desiccating arm of the northern Chihuahuan, he had heard far worse stories. Sometimes search-and-rescue crews found lost hikers rambling and incoherent—often they found them dead.

But on the morning of August 8, 1999, as he drove into the park's backcountry to check on a pair of overdue campers, he did not expect to find anything that dramatic.

With him was John Keebler, a sixty-eight-year-old park volunteer. That morning, Keebler had been driving along a scenic route called Desert Loop Drive when he noticed a red Mazda Protegé parked at a trailhead. An hour later, he mentioned seeing it to Mattson, who realized that he had seen the car himself, two days earlier. The ranger went into a drawer behind the visitor center's information desk, found a camping permit that the hikers had filled out, and discovered that they were three days overdue.

Mattson was hoping the hikers—a pair of East Coasters in their mid-twenties—were just extending their stay. Park visitors, after all, rarely lost themselves in Rattlesnake Canyon, the backcountry area that the campers had listed as their destination. In fact, it was rare for people to get lost at all in Carlsbad Caverns National Park. With a total area of about forty-seven thousand acres, it is the sixth smallest national park in the country, and in its sixty-nine-year history not a single person had ever disappeared there.

Back at the park's visitor center, the thermometer read ninety-five, but now it was far hotter as the ranger stepped out of the air-conditioned park service truck and prepared to head down into the canyon, where the sun reflected off the limestone walls and turned the whole place into a giant convection oven that could easily surpass 110 degrees F.

Before he started down, Mattson wrote a note for the hikers telling them to report back at the visitor center if they showed up, then left it under the Mazda's windshield wiper. Then the two men started down the trail into Rattlesnake Canyon. This was Mattson's first search-and-rescue mission, and he wanted to get it right. Only a few months earlier, he'd completed the two years of training necessary to make a major career shift, from education ranger—a job where he had spent most of his time leading tourists on tours of the caverns—to protection ranger, which meant that he was now charged with the preservation of not only the park, but also its visitors.

Keebler kept right along with him, despite his sixty-eight years. Mattson was glad to have him along. The older man had been volunteering at the park for fourteen years, knew the desert, and would provide an extra pair of eyes.

After about ten minutes of steady hiking, Mattson told Keebler to continue down the trail without him. The ranger broke off a few hundred yards to the left, toward the canyon's west rim. From there, he'd be about 675 feet above the floor and have a good view of the terrain below.

Sure enough, he spotted the glimmer of a maroon-and-green tent almost the moment he reached the lookout. It was right at the canyon bottom, about a half mile away as the crow flies and 250 feet from where the entrance trail spilled into the canyon.

Mattson yelled for Keebler to wait before proceeding down. The sight of the tent so close the exit trail made the ranger uneasy. "I didn't know what was going on," he later recalled. "I was thinking, you know, Why were the campers late if it was that easy to find them?"

Twenty minutes later, they reached the canyon floor. Eons of flash floods had left the bottom covered with smooth, sun-bleached stones the size of footballs. As the pair made their way toward the campsite, the rocks clacked hollowly and swarmed with heat.

"Let me go in front of you," Mattson told Keebler when they were a few hundred feet away. The campsite ahead of them lay still and seemingly empty, so much so that the feeling Mattson had up on the overlook hardened. He entered the site cautiously, with his senses elevated.

Camping supplies were scattered around the tent in what looked like a debris field: a portable cooking stove, food wrappers, a dirty sock, hiking boots, an empty Gatorade bottle, a blue bed-roll, sunscreen, a camera case—everywhere he looked there was some significant item that should have been properly stowed. A few yards to the right of the tent were the sooty remains of two fires—a luxury strictly prohibited in the tinder-dry park. The place looked abandoned, as if the campers had run off and left every-thing. Glancing to his left, his eyes fell upon a group of rocks that had been arranged in letters—an incomplete "SOS." The last "S" was only half finished.

Mattson started scanning the cliffs to see if he could locate the campers somewhere, but there was nobody in sight. He turned to take another look at the tent, then realized it wasn't a tent at all; it was what was *left* of a tent. The bottom and sides were ripped out, leaving only the rain-fly intact, and as Mattson looked closer he froze. There was a person inside, a young man, lying on his side, looking directly at him.

"Please tell me you have water," the young man said. His voice was raw, craggy.

"Yes, I do," replied the ranger. "Is everything okay?"

"Why weren't you here earlier?" the camper asked. He sounded dispirited and weary.

"Well, we're here now," Mattson said.

The ranger unsheathed the water bottle hanging on his belt and handed it to the young man. He was about five eight, with short black hair, Mediterranean skin, and a trim, athletic build. His name was Raffi Kodikian, twenty-five, from Doylestown, Pennsylvania— one of the hikers listed on the permit. As he put the bottle to his lips, his Adam's apple surged like a piston, and Mattson noticed long red scratches running the length of both of his arms. They did not look like cactus cuts. Mattson remembered that there had been two names on the permit.

"Where's your buddy?" he asked.

"Over there," said Kodikian, pointing to his right. Mattson looked but saw nothing but stones, cactus, and scrub.

"Where?" he asked again.

"Right *there*," he repeated, pointing in the direction of an elongated pile of stones about thirty feet away.

Mattson saw the stones but not the other hiker. He was about to ask again when Kodikian spoke.

"I killed him," he said calmly.

The ranger stood there for an instant, transfixed, as if he had not understood the words. They carried more information than he could digest, and he repeated them in his mind quickly. Had he heard that word correctly: *killed?* Adrenaline socked him in the chest, and he turned rapidly and faced Kodikian.

"Do you have any weapons?" he asked.

"A knife. I have a knife."

"Any guns?"

"No."

"May I have the knife?"

Kodikian calmly handed him a small folding knife, with what appeared to be blood smeared across the blade. Mattson did not take it, but instead let Kodikian set it on the rocks in front of the tent, then nudged it farther away with his foot.

Sensing no immediate threat, the ranger walked over to the rock pile Kodikian had indicated earlier. It was laid out with attentive symmetry and great care, about seven feet long, knee-high, and two and a half feet wide. Some of the stones must have weighed over sixty pounds; others, no bigger than pears, had been wedged carefully into the cracks, thwarting any glimpse of what lay beneath. Almost immediately his eyes fell upon one rock in particular. It was flat and round, and seemed to emblematically crown the right end of the mound. The more he looked at it, the more it pulled at his stomach. He carefully lifted it from the pile.

Now revealed to him was a blue plaid cloth with a rise protruding on its surface—the telltale arc of a human nose.

Mattson turned in disbelief, asking by gesture the question he couldn't yet formulate. *What the hell happened here?*

Kodikian, still inside the ruins of the tent, offered an almost inaudible response.

"He begged me to do it."

The body beneath the stones was that of David Coughlin, twenty-six, of Wellesley, Massachusetts—Kodikian's best friend. Four days earlier, they had come to the park as a stop on a cross-country road trip. The pair had camped out for the night, then become lost trying to find their way out of the canyon and eventually run out of water. According to Kodikian, that morning—only hours before Mattson and Keebler arrived—Coughlin had asked his friend to help end his pain from dehydration. Convinced they would both die, Kodikian had obliged.

———

It didn't take long for the questions to begin. Mattson radioed in a medically equipped U.S. Army Blackhawk helicopter out of Fort Bliss, Texas, then began treating Kodikian. Scattered across his arms and legs were light abrasions, rail-like cuts, and what appeared to be the red, painful-looking blooms left behind by insect bites—the small, signature wounds that the desert environment inevitably leaves on the body. What the ranger didn't recognize were more symmetrical, horizontal cuts along each of Kodikian's wrists.

"How'd you get those," he asked.

"We were in terrible pain, especially my buddy," Kodikian explained. "He was just miserable. We decided to end it, so we got the knives . . ." Kodikian paused for a moment and looked down at his wrists. "He asked me to do it for him. My knife was duller than his. That's why I'm alive."

The cuts, the ranger noticed, barely penetrated the skin.

Minutes later, Mark Maciha, the park's head law enforcement officer, strode up to the campsite. He was shorter and darker than Mattson, with a compact build and thick black mustache. The park's dispatcher had called him at his home, a bungalow just behind the park headquarters, and he had quickly gathered up a field medical kit with saline-filled IV bags, military rations, and extra canteens, then driven the four miles to the Rattlesnake Canyon trailhead. Like Mattson, he'd seen the campsite from the canyon rim and had been surprised how easy it had been to find.

"When I arrived at the campsite, Lance told me Kodikian's

story," he later recalled, "and at the time I didn't think he was lying. But later on I had a difficult time believing it."

In his twenty years of park service experience, most of them at desert parks, including Death Valley, Maciha had never heard of a lost hiker killing another out of mercy. But seeing Kodikian there beneath his ragged tent, haggard as a castaway, his only thought right then was that he needed help. Kodikian, he concluded, was dehydrated; his skin was dry to the touch and three times, when Mattson tried to give him some more water, he vomited—a sign that his water-deprived body was unable to absorb it too quickly. Maciha solved this problem by running saline directly into his bloodstream through an IV. Afterward, there was little for the rangers to do but keep their patient calm and wait for the Blackhawk. It was then that Maciha's doubts began to take hold.

"Where're you from?" the older ranger asked Kodikian.

"Pennsylvania," replied Raffi.

"Oh yeah? What part of the state?" Maciha asked.

"Town called Doylestown. Near Philadelphia."

"The weather out there sure is different. It's so green."

"Yeah," Kodikian said. "How long before that chopper gets here?"

"Not too long."

"Man," Kodikian said, irritated. "My grandmother can fly a Blackhawk faster than those army boys can."

"Hey, they're en route," Maciha said. "Let's just hang tight with me a little bit here."

Maciha fell silent. The conversation would later haunt him. Victims of heat and dehydration were often delusional and inco-herent, but Kodikian's level of awareness seemed, if anything, high. He was nowhere close to the worst case the ranger had seen, and the comment about the Blackhawk was unsettling. *Nice sense of humor for a guy who had just stabbed his best friend,* he thought.

The Blackhawk finally flew in at about four-thirty and touched down a few hundred yards south of the campsite. Raffi Kodikian was airlifted to the Carlsbad Medical Center, thirty miles away, where the questions would only mount. Waiting at the hospital was Gary McCandless, chief of detectives for the Eddy County Sheriff's Office, along with Roswell FBI agent John Andrews, who was called in because the killing took place on federal land.

"They brought Raffi in," recounted McCandless, the surprise still in his voice, "and I noticed right away when he came off the aircraft that he was in pretty good condition. Not what I was expecting when they talk about dehydration and stuff like that. He was very sharp, he was coherent. He talked well. He talked a lot about how hungry he was. He talked about how glad he was to be out of that canyon."

McCandless and Andrews had high hopes that Kodikian would tell them what had happened in Rattlesnake Canyon. How had he and Coughlin become so lost in a landscape where a climb to the highest peak would have revealed signs of civilization in almost every direction? Why hadn't he shaken his buddy by the shoulders, told him to hang in there and tough it out? And, if they had tried so hard to slash their wrists, how come the cuts were so superficial?

But moments later when the investigators approached him for an interview, Raffi Kodikian would no longer be talking. He invoked his Fifth Amendment rights. It would take him only an hour later to recover and be released from the hospital, and as he walked toward the door to leave, an officer from the Eddy County Sheriff's Office would arrest him for the murder of David Coughlin.

It would turn out that Kodikian was an aspiring writer and journalist. He loved travel and adventure, and hoped to one day pen tales of his own, perhaps in the vagabond vein of his idol, Jack Kerouac. Some would wonder if a story he wrote while lost in the desert was too perfect to be true.

2

Shade comes small in Rattlesnake Canyon. The tallest thing that casts a shadow near the spot where Lance Mattson found Raffi Kodikian is an island of brush that sits in the creek bed about fifteen feet from the campsite. Since the bed is almost always dry, calling the brush stand an island is a stretch, but it's the only place where you can study Dave and Raffi's final campsite relatively free from the harassing desert sun.

The day after Kodikian was rescued and arrested, there were nearly a dozen crime scene investigators perched on the edge of the island. Leading the group was Capt. Eddie Carrasco from the Eddy County Sheriff's Office, and John Andrews from the FBI, who had met Kodikian the day before at the hospital. With them was Jim Ballard, Carrasco's second in command, two examiners from the state office of the medical investigator, a ranger from the National Park Service, two agents from the U.S. Border Patrol, and two anthropologists from the University of New Mexico, who'd been called in because they were experts at excavating shallow graves.

Spread out in front of the team over a quarter acre were forty-some-odd items, including David Coughlin's buried body. All of the disarray that Mattson and Maciha had noticed the day before—the food wrappers, the socks, the ripped-up tent—had now become much more than a random scattering of gear cast off in what appeared to have been a struggle for survival. Even the smallest item was potential evidence, its nature and placement a cipher that, when unraveled, could either support or refute Kodikian's sparsely detailed claim about what had happened.

To preserve the crime scene, the sheriff's office had closed down the entire canyon the night before. Deputies had been posted at every entrance and exit, guarding them in shifts. Even now, tantalizingly close to the evidence, none of the investigators ventured in too far. They still needed a search warrant, and so the team stood on the island, making a list of everything in view. As the team called off the items, Eddy Carrasco radioed them to a deputy a mile away at the trailhead. The deputy, in turn, radioed everything back to the sheriff's office in Carlsbad, where Gary McCandless typed them up on the warrant. This is exactly what Carrasco and his men saw:

1 pair of men's plaid underwear
1 pair white socks
1 black knapsack
1 dark brown T-shirt with white lettering
Black nylon straps of various sizes
2 red multipurpose knives, one with an open blade

Assorted writing pens and color markers

1 black-and-turquoise knapsack

1 red leather camera case

1 black nylon camera case

1 green-and-maroon nylon tent

2 pairs brown hiking boots

1 blue-red-and-white-plaid shirt

1 small green pillow

1 black pocketknife, single blade, with what appears to be
  blood on it

1 Leatherman-type multipurpose tool/knife

2 black nylon Leatherman tool carriers

1 cassette case with cassette inside

2 boxes of poker cards

Several small boxes of matches

3 stainless steel pans

1 clear Tupperware-type container

2 dark green plastic plates

2 dark green plastic bowls

1 purple vinyl case

1 yellow net

2 plastic water bottles

1 plastic grocery bag with unknown contents

2 hard plastic containers

1 carabiner—rock climbing equipment—rope guide

1 black-and-gray article and 1 black plastic article (appears to
  be camera attachments)

1 purple-green-and-tan nylon canvas

1 blue sleeping bag

1 gray plastic tarp
2 purple nylon tent cases
1 green sponge
2 blue foam sleeping-bag pads
1 pair sunglasses
1 small butane burner

Logging the items in the heat was tedious work, but the sheer number of objects that could potentially be evidence was promising. This did not include the items—such as the knapsacks—with hidden contents. While they reeled the list off into the radio, Carrasco's second in command, Jim Ballard, panned a video camera over the site. A standard crime scene procedure; later on they would get an unwanted lesson as to why.

After logging everything, there was nothing for the investigators to do but seek shade in the saltbush and wait for the warrant. Once that arrived, they could study the scene more closely and bag everything. As the team sat quietly in the heat, they couldn't avoid looking at the cowboy grave. It was right in front of them, the tragic anchor of all that clutter, and a reminder of the worst part of the job still ahead. They knew that later in the afternoon they would lift the stones one by one and see a young man who they suspected had literally been a knife's edge away from being the kind of person that cops, rescue workers, and rangers like to encounter more than any other: a survivor.

Eddie Carrasco, who'd been a cop for twenty-five years and had come from a family rooted in the region since the Mexican era, wondered just how close to death Coughlin had been before Kodikian expedited his demise. He'd once worked with a thirty-three-year-old woman who'd been kidnapped, raped, then shot five times and left for dead in a riverbed. She'd crawled out of the riverbed, hung on until help arrived, then gone on to recall so many details about her attacker that he was easily identified and put away. Coughlin had been just twenty-six, and his friend had walked out of the hospital in just over an hour.

After exhuming Coughlin's body, the plan was to airlift it out on a U.S. Customs Service helicopter, which was due to arrive anytime. The one consolation to this grim task, however distasteful the context, was that the chopper would also be bringing lunch, and by now the team was hungry. Whether or not anyone actually said it, the phrase "Where's that damn chopper?" was not far from their minds.

The customs chopper finally showed up around two P.M. Once again it was a Blackhawk, but this pilot approached much lower than the fellow from Fort Bliss had. By the time Eddie Carrasco saw the danger, it was too late. He and his entire CSI team watched helplessly as the pilot, angling for a landing spot, cruised less than fifty feet directly over the campsite.

"They came in there and boy, when they went over that campsite, it just scattered stuff all over the place," recalled Carrasco. "Some of the stuff remained intact, but we saw shoes, knapsacks— I mean they just took off. As a matter of fact a piece of gray tarp, I believe, just utterly went up in the air and followed the helicopter to where he landed about thirty yards from where the actual campsite was. I mean, the suction from the actual helicopter blade just picked it up."

It was a detective's nightmare. To say that the crime scene had been contaminated would be a gross understatement: it had more or less been destroyed. The items, now spread out across twice the area of the original scene, no longer had any relational value. Any suggestive patterns within their overall placement were gone forever. If their disposition had hinted at a struggle, a cover-up, or the truth exactly as Raffi had said it, no one would ever know. And if the case were to go to trial, a defense attorney could use the incident as a powerful tool to cast doubt on how the scene was processed.

Another detective might have gone into a rage, but Carrasco was known for his poise and reserve. Recovering from the shock, he did the best he could to minimize the impact by ordering Jim Ballard to videotape the evidence once again, post–customs helicopter. Since they already had video of the intact scene, they could use the second tape to assess exactly what had been moved and where. The tapes wouldn't be a substitute for studying an intact scene, but together they'd have a significant degree of preservative value. So Jim Ballard sighed, got back behind the camera's eyepiece, and the two men started sifting through the new, rotor-washed evidence field.

And that was how they found the journal.

It was lying on the weatherworn rocks of the canyon floor, a few feet from the campsite, its pages blown open by the same metal wind that had lifted it from wherever it had been hiding. It was a student's notebook, made by Mead, the kind of 8 x 7 spiral pad that millions of American college students carry to class every day. Carrasco knelt over it, his curiosity vanquishing the dejection he had felt moments before.

Twenty-four pages in all had been written on, and at first glance there appeared to be two distinct styles of handwriting. Most of it was written in a masculine chicken scratch; the other style—more rounded, vertical, and feminine—appeared on only two pages, both of which were signed "David Andrew" at the bottom. Many of the entries were dated. It appeared that both boys wrote in it over the course of their road trip and ordeal in Rattlesnake Canyon, right up to the day that Coughlin was killed.

Combined with statements Kodikian would later make in court, it was either the gripping account of a road trip gone horribly wrong or one of the greatest written alibis ever created.

"We made plans to have Dave pick me up @ 3:00 from work. At 2:30 He called to say he'd be late. Dave Dave Dave . . ." read the first lines. They were dated Friday, July 30, 1999—ten days earlier.

3

Dave Coughlin had a good reason for being late that Friday. For him, the road trip he'd been planning with his buddy Raffi was more than a pleasure ride; he was moving to California to attend graduate school, which had been the whole reason for taking the trip in the first place. While Kodikian waited for him at his office job in downtown Boston, Coughlin was twenty miles away in Norfolk County, taking care of all the final details that come with a cross-country move.

There were more details than he'd imagined; he was well dug in to his community. He'd grown up in the town of Wellesley, home of the famous women's college, and had stayed in orbit of the town most of his life. The only time he'd ever left for an extended period was to attend a college just a few hours away in Amherst. He was the kind of kid nearby Boston was built on: Irish Catholic, and proudly working class. His father worked for an off-shore clothing manufacturing firm; his mom did bookkeeping work in a local doctor's office. After graduating college with a degree in environmental science, he had come right back home and taken a job working at the town hall. *This is a great place to live,* he'd often told people; *someday I wouldn't mind dying here.*

But that was a lifetime away, and first he had goals to fulfill, beginning with a higher education. So that morning he stood in a driveway outside an apartment building in the town of Milford, forcing himself to part with the woman whose name was all poetry: Sonnet Frost.

When he'd met her eight months earlier in a local bar, he'd naturally wondered if she was related to the poet; she wasn't, but she *was* the daughter of a pair of literature lovers. She had wavy brown hair and green eyes, and didn't stand much higher than his shoulders. He was a bearish guy, nearly six feet tall, with umber hair and eyes so brilliantly blue that they contrasted with the overall subtlety of his face, which was gently defined, ruddy, and decisively Irish. He was a bit stocky, but beneath the stout was plenty of muscle. He'd been working out for the past six months, and was in the best shape he'd been in since high school.

Standing with them in the driveway was Frost's five-year-old son, Daniel. As a single mother, Frost had been reluctant to introduce her son to a man whose future in their life was uncertain. Coughlin had begged to meet him every time they spoke, but she'd held off for two months. When she finally introduced them, she immediately regretted waiting so long. Coughlin and Daniel took to each other immediately, and he'd had been coming to the apartment to stay with them ever since. At the end of the street was a

New England pond, and over the past few months Dave and Sonnet had taken to sitting on its edge at dusk, talking and watching Daniel throw stones into the darkening waters.

Now, wouldn't you know it, he was leaving.

She'd felt as if she'd been robbed when he told her he was moving to California, but she understood his reasons. He needed to fulfill his goals professionally. They'd taken a trip up to Maine a few weeks earlier, walked together on the rocky beaches, held hands tight, and tried not to think of his move to California as the end. They had even talked about the possibility of her and Daniel joining him out West, or of his returning to Wellesley after he had his degree. But they were realists and decided to just play things by ear.

Neither one of them wanted the pain of a prolonged good-bye, so they made it fast. She had to get Daniel to school; and before meeting Raffi he had to pick up a few items in his old apartment, drop off the keys to his office at the town hall, and say good-bye to his folks. After embracing, she got into her car, he got into his, and they drove off in separate directions. In her last memory of him, he's in her rearview mirror, giving her a final wave until his red Mazda turns a corner.

––––––––

It wasn't until about four o'clock that Dave finally made it into Boston. In spite of the delay, Raffi had left work early and gone to a nearby video arcade to wait for Dave and play his favorite game, NFL Blitz. When Dave finally showed up, Raffi threw his backpack into the car and jumped into the passenger's seat, and they pulled out into the downtown traffic. It was a high-five moment, the culmination of weeks of planning and expectation. Raffi summed it up in the margin of the journal with a single phrase: "It was in the bag." Many of his entries during the road trip would ring with the same brevity. Since it was a travel diary, a text born in the moment, what he didn't write down, naturally, was the past.

They'd known each other nearly five years. That wouldn't be much to the park-bench bookends in Simon and Garfunkel's song, or even to younger buddies who've stuck it out since childhood, but they would have bet their bond against any other that summer. During those five years, their friendship had outlasted geographic separation, college graduation, career woes, and the greatest test of male friendship of all—relationships with women—which is precisely how they met in the first place.

Back in 1991, Dave was a freshman at the University of Massachusetts at Amherst, where he lived in a single room at Orchard Hill, a towering brick residence hall on the edge of campus. It had all the architectural charm of a state prison, and it might have felt like one if it hadn't been coed. One of the young women who caught his attention lived on the same floor as him, a petite, auburn-haired freshman psychology major from New Jersey named Day Decou.

"Dave hadn't had much luck with girls in high school," said Kristen Fischer, a friend of his since childhood. "He had been attracted to several, but had kept his crushes quiet. He was shy. He always ended up being their friends."

Things began that way with Decou, but the connection quickly deepened into what became a milestone for him—his first serious girlfriend. He'd been dating her for about two years when, in the fall of '94, she asked him for a favor: a friend of hers from high school was returning from a year abroad to resume her studies at

Boston University, and she needed to find an apartment, fast. Since Coughlin knew the Boston area best, Decou enlisted him to help her find one. And so just a few weeks before his junior year, he found himself driving around town with two attractive women, happily playing the boyfriend come to the rescue.

He found Decou's friend, Kirsten Swan, easy to help. As he sportingly chauffeured her from one apartment to another, he got to know her better and liked what he saw. She was an English major, literate, worldly, and confident after having spent a year abroad. Swan's looks, slightly reminiscent of her name, didn't hurt either. She was fair and flaxen-haired, with light-as-air arms and sleepy blue eyes, spaced just far enough apart to whisper of an old film beauty, like Harlow or Dietrich. He even offered up his parents' house, where the three of them stayed on their excursions into the city. By the end of the weekend, the mission was a success: they found her an apartment on Massachusetts Avenue, about half a mile from BU.

Dave and Day drove back to Amherst, and Kirsten settled into her new digs. A few months later, she called them with a story they could relate to: she was seeing a guy who lived in her building.

Raffi, a sophomore journalism major at Northeastern, had been living on the fourth floor for about a year. Much like it had been with Coughlin and Decou, Kodikian and Swan had run into each other around the building and the neighborhood, and the encounters evolved into a steady romance.

Raffi was more confident when it came to women. He'd dated several girls in high school, and his dark looks, wanderlust, and liberal sensibilities gave him a bit of a bad boy appeal. (It was the kind of image that Coughlin, a preppie when it came to style, would rib him about later.) Raffi had shoulder-length hair that he wore in a ponytail, and girls would often make envious remarks about it. He was also a good talker who quoted Shakespeare and Kerouac and loved foreign films, but he did more than talk when it came to his ideals. He'd worked for the Clinton campaign during his freshman year, and he'd gone to Armenia the following summer to help rebuild after the devastating earthquake.

The next time Coughlin and Decou were in the city, they dropped in on Swan and Kodikian, and that's how Raffi and Dave met.

"We immediately took to each other," Raffi would later say. "Very similar people, very similar senses of humor."

Dave was a big fan of the TV show *Cheers*, and when Raffi invited him up to his apartment, he was floored to see that Kodikian had every episode on tape. (Both of them were also huge *Seinfeld* fans, and they could sit at a bar, flipping their favorite lines and episodes back to each other.) One of Dave's favorite things to do while listening to music was to play air drums, and he was also impressed when he saw that Kodikian had a real set, which he occasionally played in a local band. He also had a pair of exotic pets, two boa constrictors named Gizelle and Severrogh that lived in a pair of elaborate cages that he'd designed and built himself.

There was no doubt about it, Dave thought after that first meeting, Raffi was a cool guy.

Dave and Day broke up shortly after their visit with Kodikian and Swan. It was amicable; they remained friends, and Dave stayed in touch with Kirsten Swan. He'd drop in on her to see how she was getting along in Boston whenever he came down from Amherst. He was like a big brother, she'd tell people, the guardian angel who had helped her settle in Boston.

Raffi found it impossible not to like it when Dave showed up. There he'd be in the doorway, a big, happy, Irish bear.

"He had this customary greeting," one of his friends remembered. "It was fast, like, 'Hey-howyadoin'-what'shappenin'-what'sgoingon?' Then he'd move on to something else before you could answer."

The trio would go out to a movie, a bar, or a party, and by the end of the weekend Kodikian was always a bit sad to see him head back to Amherst. He wouldn't have minded seeing more of Coughlin, but geography simply didn't permit it.

That changed in the spring of 1996 when Coughlin graduated. He moved back home to Wellesley—only fifteen minutes away— and was coming into the city almost every weekend. He'd call Kirsten or Raffi, and depending on what their plans were, hang out with one or both of them. But as time moved on it was Raffi he called more and more.

"Dave and Raf were always together," said Jeff Rosen, a friend and co-worker of Raffi who had spent a lot of time with both Coughlin and Kodikian in the past two years. "The first time I met Dave was at Raffi's house. He had fired up the grill. It seemed like Raffi had known Dave forever."

In the summers, they'd barbecue at Raffi's place, go to Red Sox games, or take Raffi's Jeep off-roading. In winter, they'd go snow-boarding or catch a hockey game. They went to movies constantly. Kodikian was a huge movie buff; he had a giant *Pulp Fiction* poster in his apartment and usually knew what to see. Dave was a voracious sci-fi fan who read books with the kind of stylized covers that might make Raffi shake his head, but he'd humor his friend. One time Dave talked Raffi into driving forty miles just so they could see the trailer for the long-awaited *Star Wars: Episode I: The Phantom Menace*.

Most of the time they just hung out like any other college kids. There were literally a million students their age in greater Boston. They'd drink beers and shoot pool at the local pubs, all the while busting on each other over work or girls. Raffi was the more talkative of the pair, the man of words, and Dave was content to let him take center stage.

"Dave would sit there like he wasn't even listening," Rosen remembered. "He'd be nice and quiet, then he'd get ya."

Nobody who knew both men would ever recount a single argument, not even a petty spat.

"They were a good match," Craig Lewis, a friend of Raffi's from college, said. "There was never any conflict between them when I was there; I never heard Raffi complain about Dave. Actually, sometimes *I* was a little upset, because Raffi would be going off four-wheeling, and I'd be like, 'Oh, dude, can I come?' And he'd be like, 'I promised Dave that he could come.' "

————

In 1947, a twenty-five-year-old printer's son from Lowell, Massachusetts, slapped on a rucksack, turned up his thumb to a rainy eastern sky, and hitched his first ride west on a journey that changed his life. He wandered back and forth across America's vast road network for almost two years, a postwar Huck Finn adrift on an asphalt Mississippi he affectionately called the "superslab." He kept a journal of his adventures, writing down everything he saw, everyone he met, and everything he felt in a breathless, jazz-inspired prose that echoed with the rhythm of the road itself. When he published a novel based on it ten years later, *On the Road* became an American classic almost overnight. It forever changed the way Americans thought of their highways, and, from then on, the road trip became more than the best way to see the country. It became a rite of passage.

Raffi idolized Jack Kerouac. So much so that in 1997, after he graduated Northeastern with honors, he loaded up his Jeep and drove across the country himself, following the glittered exhaust that the father of the Beats had left behind fifty years earlier. Millions of graduates make the same wheeled vision quest every year—a final gift of freedom to themselves before returning to the real world and finding a job.

Raffi, too, kept a journal, much of which he would later persuade some of the editors at the *Boston Globe* to publish in the Sunday travel section. In all, it amounted to over forty-five hundred words. His travelogue tended to be long-winded, a bit self-conscious, often focusing on the tedious details of his vehicle and the weather, but he was stretching his voice, and for a cub journalist fresh out of college they were an accomplishment—clips from a major metropolitan newspaper that he could use to get more assignments later.

"My biggest fear when I began planning a two-month solo trip driving across the United States wasn't that the journey would resemble a scene out of 'Easy Rider' or 'Breakdown,' " his first dispatch began. "Nor was it that I'd get pulled over in Louisiana by a cop with a grudge, or that some crazy driver would run me off the road in Tennessee. My fear was this: that the road wouldn't be everything Jack Kerouac had promised it would be."

To help him cash in on the promise, he had his black Jeep 4 x 4 and the addresses and phone numbers of Jeep enthusiasts he had befriended on the Internet. Kodikian speaks of off-roading six times in his *Globe* article, on some of the country's most challenging trails.

His very first stop was a Jeep gathering in Pigeon Forge, Tennessee, where he and one of his high school friends, Kevin Guckaven, spent three days four-wheeling. ". . . Our biggest concern was making it back from the trails in one piece—and in time for the cookout," he wrote. "After five years of worrying about due dates, class schedules, and grades, the lack of responsibility was a godsend."

After dropping Guckaven off at the Knoxville airport, Kodikian was alone, and he got lost almost immediately: "I spent that night trying to correct all the mistakes that my failing internal compass was causing me. Driving a Jeep with Massachusetts plates while lost somewhere in Tennessee wasn't the most comforting thought in the world, and before long my eyelids were feeling about as heavy as my belly was light."

After that first night in Tennessee, however, Kodikian seems to have navigated the roads, at least, without much problem. He moved on to Nashville, Memphis, Biloxi, and New Orleans, where he made the leap across the Mississippi. And it was there, in Kerouac's magnetic West, that he had his first encounter with New Mexico's desert.

It happened at White Sands National Monument, which lies about 250 miles to the west of Carlsbad, not far from the fabled Trinity Test Site. The monument is one of the Chihuahuan Desert's great wonders, 250 square miles of impossibly white gypsum sand dunes that lie over the land like an undulant sea of sugar. Kodikian pulled into the park on the Monday, July 7, with plans to tour the park and camp for a night. If he was expecting a campground with showers, bathrooms, and BBQs, he was disappointed. Camping at White Sands is organized almost exactly the way it is at Carlsbad Caverns: you get a permit, park along a scenic drive about six miles from the visitor center, then hike a mile down the trail, and pitch a tent. Raffi did all of this without incident. And then, after setting up camp, he went off to see the desert, an event he reported in his *Globe* article:

Not long after leaving, I noticed a rainstorm coming, so I headed back to camp to put the top up on the Jeep and throw my stuff under the tent. On the way, I noticed the wind had started picking up. It wasn't long before sand was in the air, and I knew I needed to move. I started to run, but by the time I was halfway there, all I saw in front of me was a sheet of white. The sand felt like a sand-blaster on my bare legs, and I had lost my sense of direction. I had to decide whether to lie down and ball up or move as fast as I could in what I thought was the direction of the Jeep. I opted to move, and when the wind let up slightly, and my legs could do it, I ran. For all I knew, I could have been heading straight into the desert. But as I came over the top of the next dune, I could barely make out the Jeep about 50 yards away. Thank God.

When Kodikian returned to his Jeep, he realized that he had locked his keys inside, but he was able get in through the zipper window at the rear. The sandstorm passed, he returned to camp, and the experience became just another colorful anecdote. He headed on to Arizona, where Kirsten Swan flew in from Boston to join him, and the two drove on to California and up Highway 1 in what Kodikian called a "tour de romance." In San Francisco, they both visited relatives and she caught a flight home, while he made a leisurely drive back across the entire country. The way back took him to more national parks in Utah, Colorado, and the Midwest. His sister, Melanie, joined him in Chicago, and the two drove on to Cleveland to visit a cousin before returning to Massachusetts.

"My trip has been caked on my tires, dripped on my boots, and seared into my memory as one of the greatest experiences I could have imagined," read the final lines of his *Globe* article. "And God willing, I'll get the chance to do it again."

———

That's my buddy, Dave Coughlin had told anyone who would listen. He's a real writer for the *Boston Globe*. He'd bought copies of Raffi's article and followed his adventures with pride—and envy. Kodikian's life had seemed a lot more interesting than his own in the summer of 1997. He had finished college two years earlier, and gone on to learn that the roads we take toward our dreams don't come with well-marked turnoffs and fast lanes.

"Environmental policy, Coughlin's chosen field, was completely inundated when he graduated," said a coworker who worked with him at Wellesley Town Hall. "It was rough. There was nowhere for him to go, so he came home and worked here for next to nothing."

His four years of struggling for a college degree earned him a distinguished and exciting position answering parking complaints. Quite often they were from citizens already unfairly burdened by million-dollar homes, summers in Cape Cod, and charity balls. The final outrage always came when they discovered a $25 ticket beneath the wiper of their $60,000 imported European vehicle, parked in a trash pickup zone.

"People would call and just scream at him, and I mean screaming. Profanities, the whole thing," said Arnold Wakelin, who was a selectman at the time. "He'd just sit there on the phone and smile, polite as can be. He never lost his cool."

It always amazed Dave how much perspective could be lost in the town where people seemed to have everything. Nobody in this town realizes how good they have it, he'd tell people. And as for himself, he had it good enough at first, living at home and getting free meals and laundry service, courtesy of Mom. Boston was right next door, and he spent most of his time there, hanging out with Raffi and Kirsten at the bars and parties, driving back to Wellesley late at night after his folks were already in bed. He knew he was spinning his wheels, but couldn't see where, or how, the change should come.

His father eventually gave him a push. According to a close friend, the two had a minor run-in over Dave's future—or lack thereof. He needed a plan, or at least his own place. He couldn't just go traipsing off to Boston every other night and come slinking back in the wee hours to the Coughlin Inn. Even though he'd expected it, his dad's criticism had stung, first because he thought he'd been making the best of it, and second because he knew his old man was right. He could do better.

So he moved out of the house and in with a friend of his, Keith Goddard, who worked at a local gas station. They got an apartment in the nearby town of Millis, and if Dave still wasn't sure where he was going, at least he was independent. Things slowly got better for him. He settled into his job at the town hall, where he was extremely well liked. He'd take whatever offhand projects needed work, and often put in long hours. One of his biggest inspirations had come just a few months before leaving. The town hall wasn't exactly the most technologically savvy place, and his boss,

Arnold Wakelin, asked him if there was anything they could use to streamline the annual town meeting.

"He brought in a laptop computer and did a Power Point presentation," says Wakelin. "It was the slickest thing. There he was running the whole thing from this little computer. He was a smart, resourceful kid."

They promoted him after that, and got him a raise. It wasn't much, but he had begun to find his place. He talked about staying at the town hall for a long time, if only he could find a way to secure a position less at the mercy of a city council budget.

––––––––

A friend of Dave remembers that one day he showed up at his house with a videotape, coolly put it into the VCR, and grinned proudly as he watched himself jumping out of an airplane, tied tandem to another skydiver.

"I was blown away," said the friend. "He never once mentioned that he wanted to skydive. But he was like that. He didn't talk much about doing things, he'd just do them."

California was the same way. When he took a week off work in May of 1999, he told his coworkers at the Town Hall he was going out west on vacation, but it was, in fact, a well-planned scouting expedition.

He'd heard about the Donald Bren School of Environmental Science and Management through some of his old professors and classmates. It was a brand-new school, attached to the University of California at Santa Barbara, and its two-year master's program promised the kind of hands-on, field-oriented training that got students jobs. The fact that it was fifty yards from the beach, housed in a space-age building surrounded by palm trees, didn't hurt, either.

But there were some catches: to be eligible for the program, he needed to establish California residency first, which meant that he'd have to live in the state a year before starting classes. There was also money. His parents could help him out a little, but he'd still need to work and save as much as possible. He talked it over with his dad, who suggested that he fly out and take a look. He caught a flight out west on May 18, booking it in the evening so he could catch the afternoon opening of *Star Wars: The Phantom Menace*.

Coughlin didn't go to California on his scouting expedition alone; Kirsten Swan, who had relatives there, went with him. She and Raffi had moved into an apartment together on Boyleston Street, not far from Fenway Park, but as often happens with college romances, they grew apart after graduation. During the rougher patches of her relationship with Raffi, Swan had occasionally turned to Coughlin for advice and consolation, and by the time she and Raffi finally broke up, she and Dave were closer than ever.

I'll distance myself from her if you want, Dave told Raffi, but Raffi said he didn't have a problem with it. Coughlin, after all, had known her first, and the breakup was amicable. Raffi moved into an apartment in West Roxbury, and he and Kirsten had agreed not to see each other until they'd both moved on emotionally. By the end of 1998, they were all hanging out together again, as friends, and the three of them even took a trip down to Philadelphia in December to spend New Year's with Raffi's family and watch the annual Mummers Parade, a rollicking procession of twenty-five thousand costumed celebrants that's Philly's answer to Mardi Gras. Raffi's sister, Melanie, would take a memorable photo that day; in it the three of them lean into the street as if blown back by a happy wind. Raffi and Kirsten fill the foreground while Dave peeks out from behind Kirsten's hair with smiling eyes.

In California, the only ones in the picture would be Dave and Kirsten, but Raffi knew about the trip and so did Dave's girlfriend, Sonnet Frost, and neither of them voiced any concern. Dave and Kirsten had been good friends—and nothing more—for as long as they could remember. She would be an assuring anchor for him as he surveyed the palmy landscape and tried to envision how his future would play out there. And sometime during that week, as the two toured the Western Riviera and talked it over, Dave tasted a life he wanted more of.

He came back a week later and immediately gave notice at the town hall. The dream of the West had caught him. In two months he was moving to California.

———

Packing up his car, quitting his job, and speeding off toward the setting sun was precisely the type of the adventure Raffi would approve of, and Dave immediately suggested he come along for the drive. "God willing, I'll get the chance to do it again," were the ending words to Kodikian's *Globe* article, and now here was that chance, with his best friend. But Raffi wasn't as free as he'd been back in the summer of '97.

I can't, he told Coughlin. I have no vacation time left.

It was agonizing, because Dave's offer came right when Raffi felt as if he was spinning his wheels, and looking for his own next move. Thirty years ago, Raffi's starting point after college might have been one of Boston's large newspapers, the *Globe* or the

Herald, but a bachelor's degree in journalism—or even a master's degree—carries little weight these days when it comes to landing a starting position at a first-tier publication. Major newspapers almost never hire anyone without at least five years of experience, no matter how educated they are. After graduation, the only way Kodikian could have worked in journalism would have been if he left Boston for a smaller market, which would have meant leaving his girlfriend, the town he loved, and many of his friends. Instead, he took a job in the correspondence department of Massachusetts Financial Services, one of the biggest corporations in Boston. After an adventure on the road that he shared with hundreds of thousands of readers, he had found himself writing letters to people curious about mutual funds. After two years, it was taking a mind-numbing toll, and he was eager for new direction.

To get things moving, he cut off his ponytail and met with Jerry Morris, the *Boston Globe* editor who had worked with him on his road-trip piece two years earlier. "He was not at all happy with where he was," Morris said of their meeting in the *Globe*'s cafeteria. "He wanted to quit his job and become a travel writer. He took lots of notes. He sounded serious about it. He later e-mailed me that he was thinking of doing a story about a cruise on the Great Lakes. He never pitched any other stories. He was taking notes during our whole conversation. He even taped our conversation."

Morris warned Kodikian about some of the pitfalls of travel writing, mainly that it pays almost nothing, especially for beginners. Kodikian had been paid about $350 for his road-trip story, which translates into about 8 cents a word. Newspapers are infamously cheap when it comes to paying freelancers. Magazines, on the other hand, pay anywhere between 50 cents to $2.50 per word, and at one point Kodikian also arranged an interview with an editor at *Boston Magazine*, John Marcus, who had talked to one of his classes at Northeastern.

"He mentioned wanting to write something in the spirit of *On the Road*," remembered Marcus, "I told him, well, that's the story that every kid just out of college wants to write, so he'd be better off pitching something else."

Moving was also another option Kodikian was mulling over. He told his friend Jonathan Pape, who he had interned with at the *Globe*, that he was thinking about heading off to Denver—the same town that Sal Paradise, the character that Kerouac based on himself, is inexorably drawn to in *On the Road*. But unlike Coughlin, he had not reached a decision.

If Raffi couldn't accompany Dave on his adventure, he could at least help him plan it, and the two mapped it out over beers and games of pool. The route Dave decided on ended up being almost identical to the one Raffi had taken in '97, a swing through the South.

A week before Dave was to leave, Raffi, Kirsten, Sonnet, and a few of his other friends took him out for a going-away dinner at an Italian restaurant in Boston's North End. It was a bittersweet occasion, as Dave realized that he wouldn't be seeing his friends for a long time. He fought off the sentimentality by rallying around the adventures he would have on his trip west. Raffi listened while Dave talked about visiting Graceland, New Orleans, and Austin. The excitement in his friend's voice piqued his wanderlust.

What the hell, he told Coughlin. I'll ask for some time off. At such short notice, it's a long shot, but they might just let me take some unpaid leave.

A few days later, he called Dave at the town hall. He had talked his supervisor at MFS into letting him go.

"David was ecstatic when Raffi called to say he was coming with him," said one of Coughlin's coworkers. "He put the trip off two weeks just so Raffi could come."

4

The friends reached the outskirts of Philadelphia at about ten o'clock. Since Boston, there had been "traffic out the yin-yang," Kodikian would later write, but the congestion of the seaboard's weekend traffic dissolved as they passed the city and approached their first night's destination: Raffi's hometown of Doylestown, in Bucks County, Pennsylvania.

Bucks County has some of the greenest land in America. It lies about fifteen miles northwest of Philadelphia, in a region filled with luscious farms, riparian forests, rolling hills, six wineries, and twelve covered bridges that give Madison County, Iowa, a run for its money. Every fall, newspapers and magazines all over the Mid-Atlantic pick it as one of the top places to see fall foliage, and tourists from across the country drive through by the thousands, charmed by hot-colored elms and dogwoods. The county was origi-nally named after Buckinghamshire, England, which has a similar terrain, but it's a running joke in Pennsylvania that the name comes from all the money of its residents.

Doylestown sits right in the middle of the county. Like Wellesley, the town is prime real estate; the houses along its wooded lanes represent some of the highest average home values in the state. Its citizens, too, have strategically embraced their main street, shoveling out the funds to replace cement sidewalks with brick and granite promenades, restoring it to the exact moment it arrived at the Norman Rockwell nexus. On Main Street, the refurbished County Theater hawks era movies such as *Rebel Without a Cause* in bright red letters, while parking meters still charge a quarter. The town is filled with art galleries, antique shops, bed-and-breakfasts, fine restaurants, and Victorian-era architecture. It's easy to see at least part of the reason why David and Raffi were friends; exchange the Charles River with the Potomac, switch Boston with Philadelphia, and you almost have the same town.

Like Dave's father, Raffi's is a businessman. When people in Doylestown need to rent something—party supplies, Halloween costumes, power saws, almost anything—they go to his dad's store, Rental World. Harold Kodikian, or "Hal," as he likes to be called, played his cards right. He opened up his first store in the nearby town of Lansdale back in the early seventies, and now runs two branches. When people come into the store, they recognize Hal by his gray, well-trimmed beard, falconlike brow, and the same dark and penetrating eyes he passed on to his son. Raffi's mom, Doris, is of slight build, with short gray hair and a warm smile.

The friends pulled into Doylestown at about ten-thirty Friday night, driving the day's last mile down a shady and narrow gravel road called Dogwood Lane, or *The* Lane, as the locals called it.

The Kodikian house lay at its very end, receded among some of the same trees that give the street its name. Unlike the house Dave grew up in, Raffi's childhood home is spacious and contemporary, a two-story with wood paneling and a large deck.

The boys came in through the back door, hoping to surprise Raffi's parents, but Hal and Doris had been waiting up. They greeted the boys warmly and chitchatted about the drive, but the friends were back out the door in minutes. They were hungry and eager to take a spin in Raffi's dad's car, a BMW Z3.

They met up with some of Raffi's old friends from high school at a local Friday's Bar and Grill, then finished off the night by shooting a few games of pool at one of the town's few bars, Kellys, an Irish pub on Main Street. "We left around 1:30," Kodikian later wrote, but as they stepped out of the bar they were still jazzed up from finally being on the road. Downtown Doylestown was mostly empty now; beyond Main Street, quiet lanes ran off into the night. Raffi swung the BMW onto a back road and stopped the car.

They knew that getting squirrelly in his dad's car was a high-schooler's game—but there they were, out in the boondocks in a high-performance luxury vehicle, a car they wished painfully they could take with them on the trip ahead. Raffi got out of the driver's seat and let Dave take the wheel, directing him into the farmland outside of town. After the lights of the town were no longer visible, they switched seats again, and Raffi opened up the engine. They raced home through the darkened farmland, seeing only the road in front of them, reveling at the thrill of speed in a void. "Had a ball on the corners," Kodikian later wrote.

The rest of the journal entries Raffi made on their road trip were brisk, as fast as the pace they kept. "Got up around 7 & jumped in the shower. Mom & Dad had coffee & toast waiting for us. She also picked some cherry & offered us pretzels—two kinds. We took the fat ones. She offered chicken but we declined," he wrote of the next morning. Raffi's parents wished they would stay longer, but almost as soon as they were finished eating they were back in the Mazda, on their way to Coughlin's sister's house just outside Washington in Gainesville, Virginia. That afternoon, reunited with her little brother, Kathleen and her husband, Mike, took the friends on their first tourist stop: Arlington National Cemetery. "It was hotter than hell," Kodikian wrote, "but good to finally see it. Afterwards we got the kids food at McD's, then got take out from Olive Garden. Picked up some rum & made Daiquiris at Katty's."

When the friends said their farewells to Dave's sister and nephews the following morning, in a way their trip was only then just beginning. No more family stops lay ahead. From then on, it would be only them and the explorative possibilities of a thousand towns.

The lure of the road is the same as it was in Kerouac's time, but the road is not. The America Raffi and David saw whisking past was arguably less innocent, and much more predictable. One of the revelations on the road today is not so much that America is wonderfully varied, but that it is so overwhelmingly the same.

Lined up near the off-ramps of almost every town they passed were the same signs: McDonald's, Cracker Barrel, the Olive Garden. It was a forest of the familiar, with the same exchangeable architecture, the same procedure everywhere. At times it felt as if they weren't really moving at all, but stuck in idle while a giant conveyor of road circulated the identical town past, again and again.

The only way to break the monotony was to leave the superslab and take some of the older highways and roads, which often still carry surprises. The small towns that we still equate with the American Dream still exist, just beyond the monolithic rind of chain restaurants, retail outlets, strip malls, and tract housing. Whenever they'd take a moment to get off the highways, they'd turn a corner and suddenly there it was, Main Street, with its old brick bank and square block of park. Too often part of its charm lay in its own decay. Every third building was boarded up, its mom-and-pop business long ago strangled by the interstate, or the population it once nested gone elsewhere. The little towns that have survived usually have one thing in common—the preservative balm of money—or they've had the fortune and foresight to position themselves successfully as a historical niche.

While the road is less arbitrary, it is much faster and infinitely more convenient. Most of the time they just bypassed the towns altogether, happily leaving their secrets indecipherable within constellations of halogen and sodium lamps that breezed past in the night. They knew that if they suddenly became too tired, there'd be a Motel 6 near the next off-ramp, or if they were too exhausted to search for a decent restaurant, there would also be a KFC, where the colonel's chicken was as reliable it was a thousand miles ago. It was a wonder in its own right, the idea that they knew what they were getting wherever they were. Getting lost was next to impossible, even on the older routes, because it was only a matter of time before they'd cross another highway.

Raffi and David didn't spend much time on the scenic routes. After leaving Dave's sister's house, they headed for Nashville as fast as they could. "The ride wasn't too eventful, save a rain that was bad enough to make us pull over," he said of Sunday's leg. "We got into Nashville around 6:00." If his reckoning was accurate, they motored a distance of about 650 miles in only ten hours— good time when you factor in gas, food, and rest stops. Not the kind of time you make on a back road, but by sticking to a major highway, like Interstate 81, and keeping the speedometer pegged above seventy.

By the time they pulled into Nashville, they were eager to leave the car. Like always, it didn't take them long to sniff out a local pool hall, where they ordered some Guinesses and food. "Immediately didn't like the bartender," Raffi noted. "He poured the beers half way to let them settle & dropped $2 on the bar. He then stood around for 5 min, far longer than necessary. One of my biggest pet-peeves."

After shooting a few games, they walked around downtown Nashville, then drove to a campground just outside of town. "I was glad that Dave liked the city as much as I did," Raffi wrote.

———

They kept up the dizzying pace. The next day, Jeff Rosen, Raffi's friend from work, got a phone call from Raffi and David. They were at a bar in New Orleans.

"They called me up to make sure I was having fun at work," he said. "They were about to cruise Bourbon Street."

That morning, they had raced out of Nashville, headed for Memphis. But instead of stopping in the city they had driven straight to Graceland and taken the obligatory tour, tarrying just long enough at the colossal gift shop for Dave to buy a postcard, which he later sent back to the folks at the town hall. With the rest of the afternoon in front of them, they decided to barrel on down Highway 55. The entire state of Mississippi had gone by in a blur of oaks and off-ramps—miraculously without a single speeding ticket. They had pulled into New Orleans in the late afternoon, found a youth hostel, and decided to call Jeff and rub it in.

In the background, Rosen could hear a television, Bob Barker's voice setting the stage for the Showdown Showcase during the final minutes of *The Price Is Right*. He quickly picked up a pen. "Whenever one of us was out of work, he would watch *The Price Is Right* and we'd bid against each other in the Showdown Showcase. We'd do that for beers. Whoever was closest without going over won beers off the other guy."

Rosen couldn't remember who won the beer that day, only that afterward, Raffi told him he had to go. "He was gonna go smoke a cigar on Bourbon Street," said Rosen. Jeff was glad that his friends were having a good time.

————

By the end of the next day, they were in Austin, Texas, and exhausted. They wanted a real bed, so they booked a room in a Motel 6 not far from the center of town, then called a cab. They were sick of driving, and wanted to knock back a few drinks in the Southwest's college capital.

Over beers at a local bar, they talked over their itinerary. They'd been making great time—they were a whole day ahead of schedule—but the pace was starting to get to them. The trip was more than half over, but all those miles seemed disproportionate to what they'd actually seen, which really wasn't much more than a few streets, bars, and tourist traps in five different cities. Their plan for the next day was to swing northwest to Amarillo and the Texas panhandle, then west toward Santa Fe. From there it would be a straight shot west to the Grand Canyon, which they were planning to see on Thursday.

As they discussed what lay ahead, Dave remembered something he'd heard during one of the many going-away conversations he'd had in previous weeks. "If you have a chance, check out Carlsbad Caverns; it's pretty incredible," an uncle of his had told him. The caverns, Coughlin now realized, were almost due west of them, which meant that seeing them wouldn't put a big dent in their Grand Canyon plan. They could simply head north on Thursday instead, swinging through Phoenix. He ran the idea by Raffi.

Kodikian thought it over. The only drawback to the plan was that it meant he would have forgo a large chunk of his (and Jack Kerouac's) favorite highway, Route 66, the famous "Mother Road," which in the Southwest lay withered and abandoned alongside Interstate 40, like a molted snakeskin a thousand miles long. He had been looking forward to seeing it again since '97, but he couldn't ignore the excitement in his friend's voice. It was, after all, Dave's trip.

Yeah, that sounds good, he told Dave. Let's check out Carlsbad Caverns.

5

Water is the ink of history in the American Southwest, and Raffi and David were now approaching a region whose story was written by a nine-hundred-mile-long river. It runs the length of eastern New Mexico, down into Texas, where it merges with the great Rio Grande. It was none other than the defining artery of the Old West, that muddy ribbon of water a cowboy was always either east or west of—the Pecos River.

Prior to the Civil War, most cowboys and settlers stayed far east of the Pecos, especially the part of it that ran through southeastern New Mexico. The surrounding desert was controlled by the Mescalero Apache, who resisted Spanish, Mexican, and later American colonization with as much ferocity and guerrilla expertise as any tribe in North America. The Chihuahuan Desert was the center of their world, their very name derived from a cactus that grew there. They knew the locations of every water pocket it harbored, and fighting them in their own desert was suicide.

Anyone willing to venture into southern New Mexico needed to be bold and well armed, and have a very good reason for being there.

There were two such men: Charles Goodnight and Oliver Loving, Texas cattlemen. At the time, hundreds of thousands of wild Spanish cattle roamed Texas, and making a fortune was a question of rounding up a herd and driving it to market. Comanche and Apache Indians controlled most of north and west Texas back then, so the traditional routes had always been east to New Orleans, or a riskier ride north into Illinois. By 1866, however, the markets in these states were saturated and the trails crowded. The markets in Colorado and Wyoming, however, were ripe for the picking, thanks to newly discovered gold fields near Pikes Peak. Goodnight and Loving knew that whoever could drive a herd to Colorado stood to make a killing.

The problem was that, come spring, the standard route into Colorado—the old Santa Fe trail—would be clogged with herds belonging to competitors. They needed a different route, one with a reliable water source, and decided that it was worth the risk to head due west to the Pecos and follow it north. They struck out in the spring of 1866 with eighteen armed men, successfully avoided Indians, and made a fortune. Afterward, their route was known as the Goodnight-Loving Trail, and in its wake, determined settlement in the Pecos Valley was under way. A year later, after Loving died from a Comanche arrow wound, Goodnight teamed up with the legendary cattleman and fellow trailblazer John Chisum, and the pair began grazing eighty thousand longhorns along the Pecos not far from what is now the town of Carlsbad.

To the Mescalero, the sudden presence of thousands of cattle and hundreds of "white eyes" on the Pecos was an outright invasion. Led by the brilliant war-chief Victorio, the Mescalero entered into a ferocious resistance that tied up settlement in southern New Mexico and west Texas for almost fifteen years. Only after the U.S. Army hired Apache guides and posted detachments at every water hole along his raiding routes were they finally able to defeat Victorio. The last battle he fought before retreating to Mexico took place in 1880, when his band rode into a trap just across the Texas border at Rattlesnake Springs. Heavily outnumbered, Victorio is said to have fought the soldiers only in the hope that he could push them back long enough to draw water from the spring.

———————

The drive from Austin, Texas, to Carlsbad, New Mexico, was 550 miles—an endlessly repeating conveyor of baked Texas flatlands and lonely, windblown ranches. By late afternoon, Raffi and David had crossed the Pecos, and found themselves speeding through Eddy County, New Mexico, which was founded by a man who had come from as far as they, Charles B. Eddy. An adventurous, stone-eyed New Yorker, Eddy came to New Mexico in 1880 and began ranching right where the city of Carlsbad now sits. He, too, fought for water, and in his case it was the Pecos River itself that he was after. Four years after he arrived, a devastating drought killed a third of his stock, and Eddy decided that the only way to survive was to use the river to irrigate the surrounding desert so it could be farmed. In 1888, he teamed up with some locals to form the Pecos Valley Land and Ditch Company, and embarked on a massive construction project that eventually brought water to twenty-five thousand acres. At the time, the area was part of the infamous Lincoln County, and if Eddy had any doubts that he was in the Wild West, he needed to look no further than his principal partner: Pat Garrett, the same man who, as sheriff seven years earlier, had put a bullet from his Colt .44 through the heart of Billy the Kid.

The pair made a good team. The combination of Garrett's western know-how and Eddy's New Yorker's flair for selling saw the creation of a town out of more or less nothing. Eddy printed up brochures he ran in East Coast newspapers, advertising of a "land of milk and honey" along the Pecos, and a trickle of settlers soon followed. Ironically, the very water they were harnessing wiped out much of their efforts in 1893, after the Pecos flooded. The irrigation system would be rebuilt and expanded in later years, but after that the residents of what was now called Eddy County decided that they could no longer base their livelihood on the rise and fall of the Pecos. Looking for a more permanent draw, they turned to the river once again, this time hawking its curative powers. A local wag had noticed, or claimed, that the Pecos near Eddy had nearly the exact same mineral content as the famous spa in Karlsbad, Czechoslovakia, and the town seized on the opportunity and quickly renamed itself after it. Soon the ads were once again flowing in the East Coast papers, but unfortunately the spa idea never quite caught on. Carlsbad found itself limping toward the next century.

In 1898, a local cowboy named Jim White noticed an unusual smoke column percolating into the desert sky, and he hiked over to investigate. Drawing near, he realized to his awe that the dark cloud was really a stream of bats—over a million of them—emerging from what appeared to be a bottomless hole in the ground. Intrigued, he returned a few days later, roped down into the hole, and discovered what he immediately recognized as one of world's great geological treasures.

"I came to more and more stalagmites—each seemingly larger and more beautifully formed than the ones I'd passed," he later told a biographer. He continued:

I entered rooms filled with colossal wonders in gleaming onyx. Suspended from the ceilings were mammoth chandeliers—clusters of stalactites in every size and color. Walls that were frozen cascades of glittering flowstone, jutting rocks that held suspended long, slender formations that rang when I touched them—like a key on the xylophone. Floors were lost under formations of every variety and shape. Through the gloom I could see ghost-like totem poles, tall, graceful, reaching upward into the darkness. I encountered hundreds of pools filled with pure water as clear as glass, their sides lined with crystalline onyx marble. The beauty, the weirdness, the grandeur and the omniscience absolved my mind of all thoughts of a world above—I forgot time, place and distance.

Once again, water had played a central role—in this case an epochal one—in the creation of the caverns: twelve million years of rainfall seeping through the limestone remains of a prehistoric coral reef that once stood on the edge of the biggest water of all— the Permian Sea. The water and limestone combined to form sulfuric acid, which gnawed away at the reef drop by drop, countless billions of teeth of time that left behind magnificent underground chambers as megatherial and as stupefying as time itself.

Nobody believed the cowboy's tall tale about stumbling through the belly of God, of course. The only man who listened was Abijah Long, a guano miner who cared little for the caves themselves. Hiring Jim White as his foreman, Long leased the land, and the two set about turning twenty thousand years of bat guano into fertilizer for Californian farms. White never lost sight of what he considered the real resource—the caves themselves. Whenever he had a free moment, he continued exploring them and gave tours to whoever asked. For twenty years, he wrote letters trying to get scientists, newspapermen, and the government interested.

When the Department of the Interior finally got around to sending a dubious inspector to New Mexico to check out White's claims, he returned to Washington a humbled man: "I am wholly conscious of the feebleness of my efforts to convey in the deep conflicting emotions, the feeling of fear and awe, and the desire for an inspired understanding of the Devine [sic] Creator's work which presents to the human eye such a complex aggregate of natural wonders . . ." he wrote in his official report.

Calvin Coolidge finally declared Carlsbad Caverns a national park in 1930. It had taken Jim White nearly thirty years of letter writing, but at long last, thanks to the most dogged booster of them all, Carlsbad was fixed on the map. Salvation had come from beneath the very desert they had fought to tame. A dying town built on flimflam, false promises, and failed ventures had finally found a great emptiness that it could sell forever.

———

It was close to five P.M. when Raffi and David finally pulled up to White's City, a cluster of tourist shops and motels that clings to the park entrance. They were road weary, nursing the dregs of a hangover from their night out in Austin, eager to find a place to camp and rest. At the Texaco station just off Highway 62/180, they asked Brian Laxson, an attendant, if he knew of any nearby campgrounds.

"There's an R.V. park, and you can also camp up at the caverns," Laxson told them. They decided that the second option, camping in the park itself, was the best choice. They'd be closer to the caves, and it would be cheaper. They hopped back into the Mazda and wound their way up the seven-mile road to the visitor center.

Carlsbad Caverns' visitor center sits atop a broad plateau—a remnant of the ancient Permian reef that overlooks the surrounding desert for miles. Getting out of the car and stretching, they saw a flat and limitless peel of rusty land, an immense griddle with a horizon that stretched all the way back into Texas. The air conditioner in the Protegé had been set on high; now they abruptly felt the Chihuahuan heat, mixed with the tarred air of the hot summer parking lot.

It was a cool seventy inside the visitor center. The day's last tourists were exiting the cave elevators, a pair of ingeniously convenient lifts that descend 754 feet straight into the Big Room, a cavern so colossal that it takes an hour to walk its perimeter. The walls of the visitor center were covered with geological exhibits and photographs of the wonders below: towering stalagmite columns, gypsum crystals suspended by threadlike stalks, flowing draperies of sandstone so intricately textured that they resembled forests, broccoli, ice-cream cones. It would have to wait for the morning.

At the information desk, a young ranger with a dark, seaman's beard was fielding questions from a line of tourists, most of them interested in that evening's bat flight—an event that Raffi and David would have wanted to see. In just about an hour, over a million Mexican free-tailed bats would begin their nightly exodus from the caverns' natural entrance—the same wondrous spectacle that had lured Jim White to the caves a hundred years earlier. Long since then, the park had constructed an amphitheater around the caves' mouth, allowing visitors to sit comfortably and watch the show unfold. At first, what seems like a few dozen bats whirl around the hole; then, as darkness thickens in the New Mexico sky, so does the bat cloud. They come out in waves of tens of thousands, the buzzing of their wings incessant as the streams grow denser and denser. Finally, they become so concentrated that individual bats lose all identity within the whole, fading into what seems to be a long, giant serpent, winding its way to the southeast, where the bats disperse to spend the night feasting on the insect blooms of the Pecos and Black Rivers.

Unfortunately, hanging around for the bat flight didn't mesh with David and Raffi's plan. Sometimes the exodus could last over two hours, and by the time it was over, it would be too dark to make camp. When their turn in line finally came, they asked the bearded ranger, a twenty-three-year-old student from Purdue University named Kenton Eash, what they needed to do in order to camp.

"The nearest place is Rattlesnake Canyon," Eash explained, pulling out a map of the park's main roads and trails. To get there, they'd have to drive about five miles down a nearby dirt road, park at the trailhead, then hike about a mile downhill into the canyon, where they could pitch a tent. The friends talked it over. So far, they'd slept in the tent only one time, outside Nashville, and they were now more than halfway to California. They wouldn't have many more opportunities to rough it. After a fast consideration, the friends agreed: they were game.

Eash gave them a camping permit to fill out, and Raffi wrote down the make and license number of their car, the number of campers, and both their names. In the box entitled "length of stay" he listed one day. When he was finished, the ranger removed the carbon copy and filed it in a nearby drawer.

The last thing Eash did was read off a list of guidelines for back-country camping. Most of them were self-explanatory, the kind of rules posted at national park trailheads across America: Lock your car, don't build any fires (use a gas cooking stove), pack out what you pack in, don't disturb any plants and animals, buy a topo-graphical map. One of the rules, however, was emphasized above all others. It appeared in a typeface that was italicized, capitalized, and underlined: "There is no water in the backcountry. So you must carry what you need. A minimum of one gallon per person per day is recommended."

After Eash was done, the pair prepared to head off and make camp. According to the list Eash had just read them, there were two things they needed: water and a topographical map. While Coughlin waited, Kodikian picked up the topo map at the cavern bookstore, then went over to the gift shop to buy water. All they had at the display shelf were pints, which meant that he'd have to buy sixteen bottles to satisfy the advisory.

He pulled three bottles from the rack.

6

Just past the visitor center's west parking lot, a swinging cattle gate marks the beginning of Desert Loop Drive, the dirt road that leads to the Rattlesnake Canyon trailhead. Next to the gate is a brown park service billboard, covered by Plexiglas, with a brief description of the local ecology, a map of the road, and the same list of camping guidelines that Eash had read off earlier. Raffi and David passed this point sometime close to six P.M. Eager to make camp, they likely paid little attention to the sign, but it's there to remind anyone passing it that they are entering an unmitigated wilderness of Chihuahuan Desert.

A "hot, sandy place" is what the word *Chihuahuan* means in the language of the native Tarahumara Indians. It is not only the largest, but probably the least understood desert in North America. Unlike the Sonoran and Mojave Deserts to the west, it doesn't look like what everyone expects a desert to look like. The Sonoran has the giant saguaro, that scarecrow of a cactus that children the world over

know from Road Runner cartoons; the Mojave has the otherworldly
Joshua tree with its spindly branches and starburst leaves, along with
the dunes and salt pans of Death Valley. None of the cacti in the
Chihuahuan get very tall, and sand dunes are rare. Vegetation car-
pets the landscape, but few plants grow more than two feet high.
Almost all of them bristle with spines. The plant most emblematic of
the Chihuahuan is the deceptively humble lechuguilla, a low-lying
cluster of banana-shaped leaves that belongs to the agave family. It
lacks the saguaro's brooding menace, but each rubbery leaf ends in a
point that can pierce denim as if it were tissue paper. Every twenty
years, the lechugilla sends up a thin, woody stalk that resembles an
eight-foot-high shaft of wheat. As Raffi and David drove deeper into
the desert, the scattered blooms stuck up from the plateau. It was a
surreal world of lonesome antennas.

The origins of that world were far to the south, in Mexico, where
a battle between land and sea had been going on for more than 50
million years. Its fronts are two mountain ranges, the Sierra Madre
Occidental in western Mexico, and the Sierra Madre Oriental, in
the East. Moist air from the Pacific, the Sea of Cortez, and the Gulf
of Mexico pushes inland from both coasts until it hits the Sierras and
rises. The air cools and condenses above the mountains, showering
them with rain, and by the time it reaches the interior there is almost
no moisture in it left. Squeezed dry by the two great ranges, it dis-
perses over an area of roughly 220,000 square miles, like a giant,
empty cup. Deserts formed this way are called "rain-shadow" deserts,
but the term is illusory. It rains only ten inches a year in the
Chihuahuan, and shadows don't get much longer.

Raffi and David knew they would have Rattlesnake Canyon all
to themselves when they arrived at the trailhead. No other cars

were parked in the small dirt lot that lies right next to the road, and it was late enough in the day to assume none would be coming.

As far as camping gear went, they considered themselves well equipped. Desert survival books devote entire chapters pondering the precise list of items, right down to individual brands, without which people should never enter the open desert. Raffi and David indeed had some of the core items, such as pocketknives, hats, sunglasses, boots, flashlights, matches, Band-Aids, and cigarette lighters. But there were key items they didn't have—a compass, a signal mirror, binoculars, a whistle, and a first-aid kit. The rest of their gear was standard camping equipment that's good to have anywhere: for shelter, they had a tent, sleeping bags, and foam pads; and for cooking, they had a portable stove, fuel, three frying pans, dishes, and some Tupperware containers. To eat, they packed a can of creamed corn, a large can of beans, half a bag of hot dogs, some buns, and a few energy bars. Among the numerous trivial items they brought in were some playing cards and a few cigars. Raffi also brought along the journal and some pens.

When they were ready to go, they locked up the Mazda, shouldered their packs, and struck off down the trail. It was all downhill, and as they hiked, every fifty yards or so they passed rock cairns—fifteen-inch-high piles of white limestone—that marked the route down to the canyon floor. Now and then the trail would skirt an overlook, and they would get a view of the terrain below. It looked like a lonely backdrop from an old western: a rocky moonscape of canyon, cacti, and bone-dry riverbed.

After about twenty minutes, they reached the canyon floor, where they stopped to rest and drink some water. They both carried a pint bottle Raffi had bought (the third was packed away with their gear), and they chugged at them voraciously. Sunset was approaching, but the temperature still clung to the mid-eighties, and they had worked up a sweat on the way down.

The terrain was now flat, and they could camp anywhere they wanted. But as tired as they were, they elected to move on. There were only two directions they could go: up the canyon, following a trail to their right, or down it to the left. The trail down the canyon—or southeast—would have been the logical choice. It's the main trail, marked on the map by a bold dotted line. The trail up and to the northwest is lightly dotted—a "primitive route" according the key.

They took the trail less traveled. Turning right, they hiked up the canyon. After about a mile, they left the trail entirely, wandering another quarter mile up a side canyon to the west. The site they finally chose was next to a rock face on the side canyon's wall, where an abutting horizontal slab of stone provided a natural bench. They leaned the packs up against it, set up the tent, and prepared to eat.

Dinner was hot dogs and creamed corn. But as soon as they started to cook the dogs, they realized they needed water to boil them in. They opened the last full pint of water they had, poured it into the pot, and lit the stove. When the food was ready they had the first meal of their new adventure, quenching their thirst with a bottle of Gatorade.

Satisfied, they kicked back on the rocks and talked. Dusk was settling in now, profoundly softening the character of the desert. During the day's heat, Rattlesnake Canyon can seem hostile, but as the night's cooling begins, colors deepen and change as rapidly as the temperature, and the earth's iron reds and the cacti's pale greens buzz and glow with an almost hallucinogenic depth. They say that if you stare at the desert around Carlsbad long enough, you can envision the time when it was all water. The Capitan Reef is there in the shapes. Stare at that lechugilla stem long enough, and after a while it becomes something tunicate, a lonely sponge rising from the ancient reef. That prickly pear cactus, you suddenly realize, is not unlike a fan coral, while mice, rabbits, snakes, lizards, and road runners dart among the scrub like fish in sea grass. The primordial liquid roof is gone, exchanged for sky, but the fundaments of form remain.

Dave pulled out his camera and took a shot of their tent, neatly set up in a New Mexico canyon, so far from where they had started their journey. The friends had come a long way—about twenty-seven hundred miles in only six days. They felt as if they were still racing down the highway whenever they closed their eyes to sleep. All that distance felt like quite an accomplishment. And there was still plenty more country to come. Tomorrow they'd get to see the caves, then head over to the Grand Canyon—wonders of nature they knew they'd remember for the rest of their lives. And there was California, which they'd make by Saturday. But thoughts of seeing the Pacific wore a wistful lace: that would quite literally be the end of the road, and they were old enough not to have many illusions. Their friendship as they had known it for the last few years would almost certainly be radically diluted by distance, time, and life's new courses. Oh, they'd promise to keep in touch, maybe even talk about taking another trip in the future or seeing each other over Christmas, but odds were that they'd never spend so much time together again.

As the sky blued into black, they chatted and passed the

Gatorade bottle back and forth, finishing it off as the Milky Way pooled bright above them, bridging the gap between the shadowy canyon walls with impossible clarity.

———

Morning in Rattlesnake Canyon has its own kind of charm. Mule deer clop over ridges, desert cottontails freeze and scatter in the scrub, kangaroo mice seem to bounce on air as they jump across the canyon floor. When the friends woke up at around eight the following morning, the animals of the desert were preparing for bed, finishing up the night's foraging before the day's heat sent them to shade.

"Leave no trace," one of the park's camping guidelines had read. Raffi and David did their best to follow it to the letter as they broke camp. They bagged up all their garbage, patrolled their gear, and as they started back to the car, they were pleasantly satisfied that the little side canyon lay almost exactly as they had found it.

It was perfect walking weather: seventy-five degrees, with a few clouds low in the sky. As the friends ambled along the canyon floor they took their time and enjoyed the rustle and hum of the desert wildlife. Dave wore his camera around his neck and kept an eye out for potential shots. So far, he'd taken far fewer photos on the trip than he'd expected, and now that he was in the West he was hoping to make up for it.

After hiking just over a mile, they came to a cairn on the edge of the riverbed. Next to it was a path through a small brush field that appeared to head toward the canyon's eastern slopes, which they remembered coming down the previous evening. They also remembered thinking that all that easy downhill going would be uphill going the next morning, so now they paused to rest and pulled out their water bottles.

There wasn't much left from the last night's hike and then boiling the hot dogs—about a half pint each. But there was a full bottle of Gatorade waiting for them back at the car, only minutes away. They polished off the remainder to fortify themselves for the climb out.

Setting off again, they followed the trail into the brush field for about a hundred yards, and were quietly surprised when it took them right back into riverbed. Another fifty or so yards later, they both started to get a funny feeling. None of the surroundings seemed familiar.

"The trail out must be somewhere back in the field, because this one looks like it just keeps on going down the canyon," they reasoned.

They promptly about-faced and paced off the entire path again, this time meticulously scanning the canyon slopes to their left as they searched for more cairns marking the trail out. But all they saw was an unbroken face of cactus, brush, and limestone boulders.

They stood at the edge of the brush field and thought it out: if they didn't recognize anything after the field, and there was no junction in the field itself, then the only logical conclusion was that the exit was even farther back, probably no more than a few hundred yards. They left the field and backtracked up the canyon floor, confident that their logic was sound. After reversing a hundred yards or so they saw something that seemed reassuring: several cairns, lying in a wide spot in the bed, a flood wash where a small side canyon joined Rattlesnake's main channel. They were looking for a junction, and the cairns sitting in this natural convergence seemed to suggest that the exit trail passed through the area as well. Knowing that their car was to the east, they resumed searching the slopes in that direction for more cairns, expecting to see one any second. But once again, they were mystified to see none.

They pulled out the topographical map Raffi had bought the night before. Published by Trails Illustrated in 1996 and designed in collaboration with the park service, it was a high-quality rendering of the entire park, made of ultrathin, waterproof plastic. On one side were extensive maps of the caverns, while the other offered a detailed topography of the park's backcountry, complete with trails, roads, springs, riverbeds, and explanatory text. The $7.95 Raffi had shelled out for it the night before had seemed steep, but now they were hoping it would pay off.

They'd both seen topographical maps before, but neither of them had actually used one, and at first glance it was intimidating. Unfolded, the map was about twelve square feet with intricate, hair-thin contour lines exploding everywhere. But they knew the basic idea: the denser areas represented rapid increases in elevation, the wider lines were more gradual. Each 2 x 2-inch square represented a square mile, and there were more than 130 squares in all. They located the road and the trailhead where the car was parked, then followed the dotted line of the access trail down to the Rattlesnake Canyon trail, which they knew they were standing right on top of. The entire trail fell within four square miles—a mere eight square inches in that vast spread of paper, and they kept squinting among the swirling lines, then looking back at the giant, three-dimensional world surrounding them for points of reference. There were about five peaks nearby, but establishing their relative height was nearly impossible while looking up at them from the constricted confines of the canyon. The map quickly became an exercise in irony: the rendering of Rattlesnake Canyon would have made a lot more sense if they weren't in the canyon already.

But they weren't discouraged, or even especially worried. One thing they were able to glean from the map was that they were in a small area, no bigger than four square miles. The trail had to be there because they had come down it the night before, and it couldn't be too far off because if they backtracked much more they'd be in the vicinity of the campsite they'd just left.

They formed a search area of about a quarter mile along the riverbed and canyon slopes and began their most careful hunt yet. At first they walked it off quickly, expecting to see the magic cairn any minute; when that failed, they tried walking fifty feet or so, stopping, and having a good look around. Occasionally they'd split up, each man pursuing an area he thought might be promising. Sometimes they'd search close to the slopes; other times they'd fall back across the riverbed for a wider view. Every new location seemed as if it had to hold the key, and when the path failed to turn up, it was almost something to laugh about. What kind of half-assed camping area is this, was the joke, but as morning burned toward afternoon they grew quieter. Rattlesnake Canyon was beginning to change.

By eleven A.M., the sun had risen above the canyon walls, and the temperature, now in the high eighties, was climbing at a rate of about three degrees an hour. Sweating, their skin hot, they retreated into the shade of a shrub bank, telling themselves that they'd look again in a few minutes, but once they had nestled into the relative coolness of the bushes, they felt no hurry to return to the hot brightness beyond. They reclined in dazed silence and tried to comprehend what had happened. It seemed incredible that only three hours earlier they hadn't had a care in the world.

———

Around noon a cloud cover rolled in, bringing relief from the sun, and something else that was far more valuable, for it was the rainy season. As fat summer drops began falling over the desert, they moved out from beneath the bush, letting the downpour cool their skin. They had already felt the first, driving pangs of thirst, and cursed the fact that they had nothing ready to collect the water. But when they noticed it was rolling off some of the larger rocks and pooling beneath them, Raffi and David quickly went into action. Kneeling down over the small puddles, they slurped up mouthfuls of gritty water, then spit it back into the empty bottles. By the time it stopped raining, they had managed to collect about three-quarters of a pint each. They took only small sips from the bottles, opting for a strategy of rationing.

Enlivened by the clouds and the rain, the friends resumed the search for the exit trail. They couldn't tell if they had gone too far down the canyon or not far enough, but both of them felt that the trail wasn't far off. Rather than risking getting more lost than they already were, they resolved to stay in the general area in hopes that rangers would soon come looking for them. Their camping permit was for only one day, and they had told the young ranger that they were planning on returning that morning.

Hunger was also becoming a factor now. All morning long they had been passing clumps of prickly pear cactus, and they couldn't help noticing the alluring, fuschia-colored fruit bells on the ends of the pads. Coughlin suggested they try eating some, and they were pleased to find that the fruit was not only succulent and rich with water, but deliciously sweet. Using their Swiss Army and folding knives, they cut more for later.

As the weariness of late afternoon set in, it became apparent that they weren't going to find the trail that day. While Kodikian set up camp on the edge of the flood wash, Coughlin made a final, perfunctory search for the trail on a nearby hill, then returned, dejected. They lay back on their sleeping pads, exhausted and bewildered.

Now facing their second night in Rattlesnake Canyon, they found little solace in the intensifying colors of the desert dusk, but it did bring cooler temperatures, which luckily didn't drop below the low seventies. They sat outside the tent, now and again chewing on the cactus fruit while they discussed their situation.

It wasn't good; they were lost in a desert with very little water. But as they saw it they had a very big card in their favor: the camping permit. Along with their car, it was tangible evidence of their presence in the canyon, a 4 x 6-inch piece of paper that was now becoming, in their minds, nothing less than a kind of contract—a receipt that entitled them to a rescue. Why else had they needed to state so much information on it, the length of their stay, their license plate number, their ages? Immediately they began to wonder about how the ranger had handled it. What if he had misplaced it? Trying to keep their spirits up, they forced themselves not to think about this possibility. They were still in pretty good shape, bolstered by the rain and the discovery of the cactus fruit.

That night, they saw something else that gave them hope.

In the near distance, immediately in front of their camp, were three successive slopes of the canyon wall. From their close perspective they looked like three mountains rising into summits, and toward midnight, they saw what appeared to be car headlights on the far mountain. The lights shone for only a few moments, but it was long enough to convince them that, if they hiked in that direction, they should find a road. The next morning, they did just that.

Before leaving, Kodikian wrote the first journal entry the pair would make during their ordeal in the park. It was a note for the rangers, in case they arrived while they were gone:

HELP HELP

We filled out a backcountry card on Wed afternoon/evening & headed down. Camped Wed, started back on Thursday morning but couldn't find the entrance to the trail leading to the car. Looked all day Thursday, slept here Thurs night, & saw headlights along mtn #3 around midnight. We're headed for that peak. (See "map" on previous page.)

We've got minimal water & have been eating cactus fruit. We need help. We headed towards what appeared to be the ranch foundation to begin. If & when we reach the car we will go to visitor's center then attempt to come back for gear—carefully.

On the facing page, Kodikian drew a rough map of the three peaks, numbering each one, and noted their time of departure, seven-thirty A.M., in the margin. They left the journal lying in front of the tent, opened to the note, and began hiking in the direction they had seen the headlights.

It was now Friday, August 6, the day they were supposed to arrive in California.

7

In 1942, the U.S. Office of Scientific Research hired Edward F. Adolph, a professor from the University of Rochester, to study exactly what happened to soldiers when they went without water in the desert. At the time, Adolph was at the head of the emerging field of environmental physiology, and with the Allies campaigning against Rommel in North Africa, the reason for the study was practical enough: the army wanted to know how far young men could be pushed before they would break under the Saharan sun.

Using hundreds of soldiers stationed in the Mojave Desert as his test subjects, Adolph, a rough-jawed army veteran himself, deprived them of water, then put them through a range of activities. He marched them, measured them, made them sit in sun and shade, stuck them in hot truck cabs and stifling armored vehicles— generally, he made them utterly miserable before giving them a drink. Some of the GIs, all of whom were volunteers, later wondered if they would have been better off fighting the Desert Fox, but the wealth of knowledge that quite literally came from the sweat of their brows is hard to understate. Adolph later published his findings from the study in a paper, "Physiology of Man in the Desert," and to this day it is the pillar of what we know about what happens to people—particularly fit young men—when they're stuck in the precise conditions Kodikian and Coughlin faced.

The reason we can survive at all in temperatures above ninety-two degrees Fahrenheit is because water—in the form of sweat—allows us to dissipate heat from our bodies and maintain a stable core temperature. It seeps out of about 2 million glands on the surface of our skin, where it cools the blood immediately beneath. Since it also evaporates quickly in the hot desert air, sweat must be continually drawn from our bodies. Depending on size and weight, 40 to 60 percent of the human body is actually water; in a person weighing 150 pounds, it amounts to about ten gallons. The hotter the air and the more strenuous our activity, the more water our system loses; and if we can't renew it, we immediately enter a downward spiral that Adolph divided into three stages.

Nearly everyone has experienced the first stage, or "mild dehydration"; it occurs when we lose between 1 and 5 percent of our water, and it often happens because people have a tendency to drink less water than they need to replace what they sweat out—a phenomenon known as "voluntary dehydration." The first symptom is usually, but not always, thirst, and we typically become dehydrated for short periods of time without ever even knowing it. As stage one progresses, however, more serious symptoms generally appear: we start to feel a vague discomfort, accompanied by sluggishness, nausea, and a loss of appetite. Psychologically, we feel impatient, irritable, partly because our hearts are beating faster in an attempt to get more blood to the skin to fight a rising core temperature. First stage dehydration is almost never fatal. Get out of the sun and drink some water, and recovery usually comes within an hour.

Second stage, or "moderate dehydration," occurs when we lose between 6 and 10 percent of our water. The blood actually begins to thicken and lose volume in this stage (unchecked, it will eventually reach a consistency almost identical to that of maple syrup). Moving viscously through our arteries, it can no longer deliver oxygen efficiently. Breathing becomes shorter and heavier, and exhaustion sets in. In the brain, second stage dehydration often translates into a banging headache and dizziness, while other neurological symptoms may include slurred speech (which can be exacerbated by low saliva levels) and tingling limbs. As the 10 percent mark nears, the oxygen problem can get bad enough to cause the lips and extremities to turn blue.

Had Adolph pushed his soldiers much beyond 10 percent dehydration (he did not), some of them probably would have died. Death can come at any time during third stage, or "severe," dehydration. Most of what we know about it comes from lucky survivors. The neurological effects are profound: deafness, hallucinations, and failing vision are typical. Potassium, which triggers muscle contractions, can reach such concentrated levels that bitingly painful spasms ensue. The tongue swells to twice its size and may actually turn black, while the eyes are so depleted of lubricant that blinking lids have the abrading effect of sandpaper. For the elderly, death is usually caused by heatstroke, but for the young and fit it often comes more slowly. Once the water levels in the blood fall low enough, the body then begins to draw it from its own cell tissue—in a sense, drinking off of itself—until a major organ fails. Usually it's the highly water-dependent kidneys.

Every indication is that Kodikian and Coughlin were still somewhere in the first stage when they set off to climb the peak on Friday morning after a day and two nights in the desert. They had scavenged water from the rain and the cactus fruit; even more importantly, they had rested out of the sun during the height of the previous day's heat. According to Adolph's research, a man resting in shade in one-hundred-degree temperatures loses only about a cup of water an hour—the slowest rate of water loss possible in such heat. By sheltering themselves in the brush, the friends had unknowingly taken the precise course of action that the professor himself would have advised.

But they were now about to do something quite different. They were about to hike in the open desert under the sun's full wrath. Had they known of Adolph's research—known what happened to his soldiers when, instead of resting, they kept marching through open desert in the heat of the day—Raffi and David almost certainly would have thought twice about heading for the peak. Adolph learned that a man marching in such conditions loses two quarts of water an hour. In other words, he expends his water reserves eight times as quickly.

———

The ranch foundation Kodikian mentioned in his journal entry was about three hundred yards south of where they were camped. It's just a ten by twenty foot square of crumbling cement wall, all that's left of an old homestead that was once part of a cattle-grazing operation. Weeds and cacti grow inside the square, and nested among them are a few rusty cans and an ornate iron leg of what appears to have been an old Singer sewing machine table. Other than the cairns marking the canyon trail, the foundation is the only sign of civilization in the canyon, a near swallowed ruin, but even that can be comforting when you're lost.

Mountain number three, as Kodikian called it, rises about seven hundred feet immediately to the west of the foundation. Although it looks like a mountain from below, with slopes rising to a crest, it is actually part of Rattlesnake Canyon's southwestern wall, and as the friends stood beneath it and gazed up, they saw cruelly inhospitable terrain. Three ridges, like gnarled fingers, rose to the summit, with the spaces in between them occupied by steep gullies. There were no trails, and both scaling options, ridges or gullies, looked bad. The ridges had gentler slopes, but they were a few feet wide at best, serrated by seemingly impassible limestone promontories and gaps. In between were the gullies, smooth in comparison, but a good fifteen degrees steeper, and shedding so much rubble that from time to time the erosion was audible in ghostly, far-off clicks of stone falling against stone. Worst of all were the minefields of daggerlike agave that peppered the slopes.

Wading into the sticky tide of creosote bushes that clung to the bottom, they began their ascent. It was slow going. Every few yards they had to veer around an impassible network of cactus, then get back on course. They could only climb in short bursts before tiring out, and each time they stopped they sucked on some cactus fruit. Looking down after they had risen a few hundred feet, they realized that if they slipped there was nothing to break their fall—except the agave. They had little choice but to keep moving forward.

When they finally reached the upper heights of the slopes, cracked and withered walls of limestone, some as high as twenty feet, blocked further ascent. They worked their way left across the slopes, looking for a more gradual route up. The left face was just as walled off, so they had no choice but to put hand to rock and climb. Each time they scaled a difficult shelf, their spirits fell as they saw another one twenty yards ahead; it was as if there were an invisible giant somewhere up ahead who kept adding steps to his staircase, toying with them. Long after they had given up expecting to see the summit, they tiredly clambered over one more ragged ledge and suddenly saw nothing above them but sky. They were at the top, the place of headlights and hope.

They saw that there was no road almost instantly.

———

Whether it was a plane, a satellite, a star, or the projection of their own hopes that they had seen on Thursday night, it had lured them in the one direction that offered the least possible help at the greatest expense. They were now farther from their car than before, exposed to the sun on barren heights that offered almost no shade. It had taken them about three hours to scale the canyon wall; according to Adolph's formulas, the trek had cost them more water than they had spent the entire previous day.

What are we doing up here? We should have stayed in camp. This is stupid, Dave said.

Let's move a little farther on, Raffi suggested. He was concerned about the frustration and hopelessness in his friend's voice. Just south of them was another ridge with a gentle slope. It was barely a climb at all, but it would give them a better view of what lay to their south. They kept moving.

The expensive climb out had bought them at least one thing: they were now no longer stuck in Rattlesnake Canyon. The terrain was still covered with cactus and loose, unsteady stones, but it was almost completely flat, and the myopic views of slopes and walls had been replaced by miles of perspective. They were standing on the same plateau as the visitor center, which lay on the opposite side of the canyon, about six miles away and a good five hundred feet lower in altitude. They should have even been able to see the square bulge of the cavern's elevator tower to their left, a small yet distinct speck of human geometry in the distance. Even closer were the twenty-foot-high water tanks that they had passed on the road in. Any of these would have told them the general direction of their car.

They saw none of them.

They continued picking their way across the plateau, until Kodikian's strength began to falter. He lay down in the paltry shade of a shrub, while Coughlin continued to survey their surroundings. He had noticed that an entirely new landscape had opened up to the south.

They were now on one of the highest points on the plateau. Immediately in front of them was another small ridge, but beyond that Dave could see the desert plains below, beckoningly flat and even patchily greened by the summer rains. If he had been stranded on an island, his position now was akin to standing on cliffs above the shore, scanning the sea for signs of a sail. And right in front of him, about four miles straight out on the plains, was all the water he could ever want: Rattlesnake Springs.

Once a favorite watering hole of the Mescalero Apache, then later the U.S. Calvary, Rattlesnake Springs is a classic Chihuahuan oasis, a limestone spring surrounded by a cottonwood grove. The park annexed the spring in 1931 to serve as its water supply, and over the years it has been teased into an irrigated network of ponds and troughs almost a mile in length. From where Coughlin stood, the oasis was the darkest spot on the horizon, with the main spring pond visible as a metallic blemish within a black nest of cottonwoods. If he looked closely, he could have seen several buildings belonging to the national park and an adjacent camp for diabetic and mentally handicapped children. Running water, telephones, and cool linoleum kitchens, just three miles away. He picked his way back through the cactus to tell Raffi the good news.

If we can make it out onto those plains, there's gotta be a road out there, he reported excitedly.

Raffi listened but made no move to get up. Exhaustion had immobilized him like a lead blanket the moment he had lain down.

If you think you can make it, go, Kodikian told him. Send back help.

Coughlin thought it over. I'm not gonna just leave you here, he finally said. And I don't want to wander out into that by myself.

He crawled under the bush and lay down next to his friend. The temperature was now breaking into the nineties, and for the moment they seemed to have given up all thoughts of escaping onto the plains. When it cooled, perhaps they'd give it another try.

They holed up on the plateau all day Friday and clung to whatever shade they could find. Ants began to bite them as they lay on the ground, and eventually they got up and moved to the biggest bush around, most likely a mesquite shrub that lives up there like a lonely old hermit. They hung their shirts in the branches to win a little more shade, but it couldn't stop the heat. By three P.M. it was approaching one hundred degrees.

8

A vulture, black and silent, soared over and began spinning above them, riding the canyon's thermals.

Soon more came, forming a desert carousel. Vultures are highly social creatures, and they often stay close to hikers and one another out of sheer curiosity. But Raffi and David didn't know that. All they knew was that they were stranded in the desert, and now the vultures were circling. It was like the script from some old movie. The vultures hover, then drop down and perch a few feet away. They wait, cruel in their patience, until you're too weak to resist. Then they move in and pick you apart—alive—one bloody string at a time.

There's no way we're going to let that happen to us, they agreed. We'll kill ourselves first. "We will not let the buzzards get us alive. God forgive us . . ." Raffi later wrote in the journal.

The environment seemed to attack them even when they were lying still, the ants, the sharp rocks, the birds, the burrs in their socks, the wind that constantly blew their shirts off the branches, forcing them to rise and reposition them. Sometime in late afternoon, Dave finally turned to Raffi.

I gotta get out of here or I'm gonna go nuts, he said.

Raffi had also had enough of the plateau, and so after expending invaluable amounts of water climbing out of Rattlesnake Canyon, they rose from the languishment of the bush, wearily put their shirts back on, and prepared to walk back into the trap they had toiled to escape.

Before leaving the plateau they sucked on more cactus fruit, but given the heat—still near one hundred by five P.M.—it didn't help much. Sweat covered them as they made their descent back into the canyon, once again struggling for footholds on the upper slopes. By the time they were halfway back to the ranch foundation, they were thirsty beyond desperation. They decided it was time to employ the oldest trick in the book: they would drink their own urine.

Drinking urine is also the biggest myth in the book, perpetuated by people who mistakenly attribute their survival to the fact that they did it. Although there are small amounts of water in urine, most of it consists of toxins, salts that the kidneys filter out because they're harmful in the first place. The urine of a dehydrated person is especially toxic and concentrated, and drinking it forces the kidneys to draw water from the blood to dilute it; in other words, urine takes more water to digest than it actually supplies.

Kodikian took off his baseball cap. They'd brought along the empty water bottles in the hopes that it might rain again. He turned the cap over, positioned it over one of the bottles, and peed. His urine was nearly as dark and concentrated as a Guinness.

He put the bottle to his lips and sipped. The acrid taste of ammonia overwhelmed him. He tried to swallow but immediately began to gag.

There's no way we're gonna be able to drink this, he said.

Dave saw the look on his face and took his word for it.

They continued on toward the canyon floor. As they got closer, Coughlin caught a glint of something they *could* drink sitting on the walls of the ranch foundation.

Are those what I think they are?

What? Kodikian said.

They look like water bottles, on the foundation. See 'em?

Kodikian squinted toward the ruin. Suddenly he, too, saw them: several plastic bottles, exactly the kind they'd bought at the visitor center, waiting right there on the ruined wall. At long last, they both realized, the rangers must have come and seen the note they'd left back at the campsite: "We're heading towards the ranch foundation . . . ," it had said. They must have left the bottles in case Raffi and David came back.

Their relief was instant. For two days, they had turned fantasizing about water into an art. How good it would feel, sliding down their throats and settling in their stomachs like subterranean ponds. Bathtubs full of cold water, motel ice machines, swimming pools, every sprinkler they'd ever run through as kids, the Pacific.

Bottles of water, sparkling on the edge of a ruin.

———

Dave had been getting weak in the legs, having difficulty bracing himself against the downhill slope, so he told Raffi to go on ahead for the water, he'd catch up. Kodikian was drained himself, but he worked his way through the scratchy maze of brush near the bottom without stopping. When he finally emerged into the open space of the riverbed, he made a beeline straight for the foundation.

The water was not there.

It had to be a trick, Raffi thought. He looked around, expecting to see someone. A twisted hiker, or a ranger with a seriously sick sense of humor who'd suddenly jump out from behind a bush and shout, "Gotcha!" Even when he realized he was alone he didn't quite believe the bottles hadn't been there.

He sat down on the wall and waited for Dave. He could hear him snapping through the brush, knocking rocks around. He didn't have the heart to yell to him that it was yet another false lead. Better that he had something to look forward to.

When Dave finally staggered over and saw that there was no water he barely had the energy to damn the mirage. His legs were seizing up on him, and he immediately collapsed against the old stone wall.

I feel dizzy, he said. Faint.

They sat awhile on the foundation's ledge, waiting for Dave to catch his breath. Two years earlier, his father had had a heart attack, and seeing his dad's brush with death had made him wonder if he'd suffer the same fate when he hit sixty; now he was worried his weakened condition might somehow speed up the genetic fuse.

There was no question where they'd go now. Back to camp was their only option, at least until they got some rest. Dave rose to his legs, which shook like a newborn fawn's. Raffi gave him a shoulder to steady himself on. They crept back toward the tent like that, limping along like the wounded comrades in arms they were. It was about a quarter mile but it seemed to take an hour. The last stretch over the wide, stony flood wash was the worst; slow, aimed steps to make sure Dave didn't step on the wrong rock and bring them both down.

This new development with Dave's legs was a bad turn, Raffi knew. If they didn't thaw out, there was no way they'd walk out of there together. How long would it be, he wondered, before his own legs gave out? He tried not to think about it, and instead focused on the ground in front of him, the swinging and planting of each step, watching Dave's feet, bracing himself for each slip. It was almost a relief that somebody required his strength. He barely looked up until they neared the campsite. When he did, wouldn't you know it, he saw a cairn that he hadn't seen before.

You remember that one? he asked Dave.

Coughlin studied it. No, that wasn't there, he said.

It was near the flood wash, the same area they had passed through half a dozen times the day before. How could they have missed it?

Like it had been with the phantom water bottles, they found themselves wondering irrationally if the rangers had placed it there while they were off hiking—a strategy to cover their fault for marking the trail so poorly to begin with. They could almost hear them snickering just out of sight, shadows in wide brimmed hats that melted into the cactus whenever they turned their heads to see them. They knew it was crazy, but if the camping permit had only been for one day, why hadn't the rangers come? What had been the whole point of filling out the piece of paper and paying their $7 to begin with? Was it just to identify their bodies?

The scene with the young ranger at the desk played through their heads again and again, his arms fumbling in the shelves, his confused eyes on the paperwork, his casual apology for ignorance. Now they saw that it was true, he really *hadn't* known what he was doing, and they had been foolish to trust him. The copy of their camping permit—the very receipt for their lives—was now buried beneath a stack of National Park Service paperwork. The no-show rangers. They hated them, yet there was no one they more wanted to see.

Despite their cynicism, the new cairn gave them hope. After all the false leads they'd followed, it was finally time for something to work. They made a new plan to rest that evening, then get out in the morning. If Dave couldn't make it, Raffi would go by himself. They were grateful to be off the sizzling plateau, back on the relative comfort of their sleeping pads and tent. They jazzed themselves up for the next day's escape; how good that bottle of Gatorade would taste! They saw it clearly sitting in the backseat of their car, an ambrosia, the calming, electric green distillation of their hope. If there were a Gatorade God, they would have promised him that if they could just get to the bottle, they'd drink the stuff religiously for the rest of their lives.

9

Raffi had a vision that night, an "awake dream" he would later call it. As he lay in the tent, his eyes opening and closing restlessly, he saw people in the canyon. They were out there in the grayness of the riverbed, busily constructing machines, devices that would transport them out of the canyon. Anxiety swept over him as he realized that he and Dave didn't have the proper tools to build their own machine. They would be left behind, like men on a sinking ship after all the lifeboats were filled.

He didn't tell Dave about the dream when they got up Saturday morning. Coughlin was feeling better. He stood up outside the tent, stretched his legs tentatively, and told Raffi he thought he still had enough strength for another try. He didn't want to be left there alone, and Raffi was grateful that he wouldn't have to face the hike back to the car by himself.

They didn't bother bringing anything with them this time. Carrying their own bodies out of the canyon would be work enough.

It took them a while to find the cairn they'd seen on Friday. They walked right past it, then had to double back before Coughlin finally spotted it again. Standing next to the marker, they took a deep breath and tried to focus on the task at hand.

If they were going to make it, everything depended on their being able to spot another cairn they hadn't seen before, then maybe one or two more. The trail would be easier to see once they were certain they were finally on it, and it would also be angled upward instead of hiding somewhere in the brush and stone-ridden flats of the canyon floor.

Slowly they turned their heads in a circle, their dehydrated brains attempting to parse the visual information, separating cactus from rock, rock from rock pile, and dirt from trail like they were staring at some gigantic stereogram. Other cairns—the same old islands that had already failed to point the way out—were nearby. Somehow they had to fit them into a pattern, a line, and they strained to integrate them into a big picture. Minutes passed. They were boys in a geometry class, staring at their final exam problem without lifting a pencil, willing it to make sense, their isolation and anger mounting as the period ticked away.

I'm going back to camp, Coughlin finally groaned. He turned and marched toward the one thing he knew he could find.

I'm gonna keep looking for a little while, Raffi told Dave. He could tell by his friend's voice that he had given up, and he, too, was beginning to feel the futility. He climbed a small rise to the right of the cairn, and looked across the canyon toward the opposite slope. They'd had a strong suspicion the trail was in that direction, but he wasn't sure of anything anymore. He'd walked many trails in Pennsylvania; they were always soft, definable tracks of brown through green. Here, where there was only a uniform melange of rock, dirt, and cacti, he could be looking directly at the trail and not even see it.

He heard Dave yelling for him. His friend was worried that he would get lost or injure himself. Kodikian returned to the camp-site, where he found Coughlin struggling to arrange some of the larger nearby stones into a pattern. He weaved drunkenly beneath their weight, dropping them down angrily, and nudging them into position with his feet. He was attempting to spell "SOS."

Let me do that, Raffi said. You can work on a signal fire.

While Raffi finished with the stones, Dave collected anything nearby that would burn and threw it into a pile. They poured what was left of their cooking fuel over it, ignited it, and as the smoke drifted away they were not impressed. It barely even rose, just lin-gered in a sticky haze on the canyon floor. Growing desperate, they threw in Raffi's sleeping bag, hoping it would generate better smoke. It seemed promising for a moment, as white, bilious plumes spewed from the fire, but it still wouldn't rise above the walls. It trailed off down the canyon like a word trapped in a throat.

The one thing they didn't burn was the journal. Sometime later that day, Coughlin made his first entry, to Sonnet Frost:

Sonnet—

Baby, write this with a shaking hand (that was not intentional I swear). I do not know what to do right now but I am in utter agony and I know you would understand. I LOVE YOU SO MUCH!!! I have barely eaten & drank since Wed. evening. Nobody is coming to help. I love you. Tell Dan if I find a heav-enly monkey I will forward one along. We had forever but now

all we have is eternity. Who knows maybe I'll get kicked out for
disorderly conduct and be able to pay you a visit. You will always
be in my heart and you will always have an angel standing by.
   Eternally yours,
      David Andrew
P.S.
I'm trying so hard to be strong right now. It's not working.

After their Hail Mary signals for help, they sought shade in the
tent. It was the hottest day yet. By midday, according to estimates,
the temperature in the canyon was nearing 110 degrees. Fighting
the heat, they cut the bottom out of their tent to circulate air
upward and to get access to the stones below, which they noticed
were cooler than the tent's nylon lining. All day long they shifted
the rocks, exchanging them for new ones as soon as they warmed,
also pulling up handfuls of pebbles and running them down their
backs, imagining that it was water.

Clouds finally started coming in during the late afternoon.
They crawled out of the tent and took turns writing in the journal:

————

From Coughlin:

Carlsbad Caverns N.P., N.M.   Sat.
   Yesterday we never found the road but reached what seemed
to be the farthest reaches of the park. Nobody has come. We
were planning to die. We mustered all our strength, we had no
food or <u>water</u>. Nobody has come.

We went back to camp in hopes that St. Nicolas would have fuckin shown up. Nobody had come. No water was left. We thought we had found the way and set off Sat. (today). Wasn't it. Returned to camp & started fire & built shelter.

I love you Mom, Dad, Mike, Kath, Beth, Kim, all kids, Sonnet, Daniel, Keith, Joe, Kir—I'm so tired. Might write later. Raf—we never gave up. See ya soon.

David Andrew

After Dave was done writing, he handed the notebook to Raffi. Do me a favor and read this, he said. I can't tell if it's coherent. Raffi looked it over, then made an entry himself:

Dave wrote it as it happened. We don't know why no one came, we only had a one night pass for Wed & now it's Saturday. But . . .

Mom, Dad, grandma, Mel, Dave, Robert & Nora & everyone—I'm sorry this had to happen twice in one year. I'll tell Harold you send your best. I love you all like you can't imagine. K, you were the only woman I ever truly loved, & that never died. To all my friends, too many to count or name right now, I love you all & have thought about you all, even long-time-no-sees. God has made my life decision for me, no more worries.

Kodikian wrote additional good-byes to his friends and family—even his old high-school journalism teacher, Kathy Nelson. There were no more words from Coughlin, but Raffi wrote for him: "Dave has asked that his remains be cremated & thrown over the edge of the Grand Canyon. I leave the handling of my remains to my family."

Coughlin was in serious pain, according to Kodikian, and they decided to end their lives together.

Raffi pulled out his Gerber folding knife, and as it gleamed in the light of the ineffectual signal fire, both he and Dave stretched out their arms and tried to slice into their veins. But out of either exhaustion or fear, they both failed to execute a fatal slice.

They realized that they were going to have to go through whatever death the desert had in store for them. How painful it would be and how long it would take was a process as darkly mysterious to them as the night beyond their fire, but they did not doubt that it was coming.

According to Kodikian, as the night wore on Coughlin's pain and resolution to die increased. Sometime near dawn, he made a request that Raffi would honor, and then document in the journal:

I killed & buried my best friend today. Dave had been in pain all night. At around 5 or 6, he turned to me & begged that I put my knife through his chest. I did, & a second time when he wouldn't die. He still breathed & spoke, so I told him I was going to cover his face. He said OK. He struggled, but died. I buried him w/love. God & his family & mine, please forgive me.
    Raffi Kodikian

After Coughlin stopped lurching, the silence came. Of all the kinds of silences—the stillness of snowfields, the hollow quiet of an empty house—none is as total as that of the desert. It is the hush of antiquity, an inverse echo that seems to embrace the countless millions of years it takes for a desert to form. It was broken briefly while he laid the stones on Coughlin's grave, and then it caved on him again from every direction, lasting another seven hours, until it was at last broken by another sound.

Lance Mattson's footsteps.

PART TWO

10

The morning after he was arrested for the murder of David Coughlin, Raffi emerged from the Eddy County jail's swinging glass door, his hands cuffed in front of him, his ankles shackled. He wore a tangerine jail jumpsuit that was almost eye-blistering in the morning sunlight. Along with a deputy, he was escorted by Chief Detective McCandless, whom he had met in the hospital the day before, and another man in a white Stetson, who was starting to take a great interest in him: M. A. "Chunky" Click, the sheriff of Eddy County himself. Although Raffi didn't know it, the two men—McCandless and Click—were cousins.

It was a short walk across the street to Eddy County's magistrate court, but there was plenty of time for a photographer from the *Carlsbad Current-Argus* to capture the moment in a photo that would wind up in dozens of major newspapers: Raffi, bright as a bull's eye, being led by the cops.

Magistrate court was held in an unimpressive, one-story brick building, half of which belonged to a small church. The courtroom itself was spare and functional, with two desks for counsels, a wood panel podium for the judge, and a few dozen metal chairs for the audience. The only adornments were two flags, one for New Mexico, one for the republic. Its two judges spend most of their time hearing relatively small-time cases: traffic violations, landlord-tenant disputes, drunk-driving tickets. Since magistrate judges have no jurisdiction beyond the county, when it comes to felonies, their job is to preside over the preliminaries—warrants, preliminary hearings, establishing bail. If they find probable cause that a felony has indeed been committed, they bind the case over to the district court.

Judge Monte Lyons was already waiting when the four men entered the courtroom. He had a welcoming, mellow face, round and lightly bronzed, but when he read the criminal complaint, his eyebrows popped to attention. Before becoming a judge, he had served on the local police force for twenty-eight years, and had never heard of anything even remotely like this.

When the deputy brought Kodikian to stand before him, he studied the young man intently, curious at the human shape an admitted mercy killer of the desert took. What struck him most, he would later say, was Kodikian's complete lack of expression.

"Mr. Kodikian, you are charged with a criminal offense, an open count of murder . . . ," Lyons said, and led Raffi through the opening phase of what was now the *State of New Mexico v. Raffi Kodikian*.

When someone is charged with an "open count" of murder, it means that the degree of murder will be decided later, either during a preliminary examination, or in the district court. Murder has only two degrees in New Mexico, first or second, and depending on which one the court eventually settled on, the judge explained, Raffi was now looking at eighteen months to life.

There was also another possibility.

"If there are any aggravating factors indicating a unique and malevolent nature to the crime . . . ," the judge explained, looking directly at Raffi, "the maximum sentence is death."

Lyons had seen men break into tears at the mention of the death sentence. Often their knees shook, or their faces chilled white. He never saw Kodikian again after this brief appearance, but he would distinctly remember the young man's particular reaction. "He showed no emotion whatsoever," he later said. "He reminded me of somebody who came in for a traffic ticket."

Lyons set bail at $50,000 cash.

————

The sheriff of Eddy County had phone calls to return when he got back from magistrate court. The story of the killing in Rattlesnake Canyon had gone out on the Associated Press newswire on Sunday evening, and now some of the regional papers were starting to pick it up. If there was one thing that Sheriff Click didn't mind, it was basking in the spotlight. Taking the stage during a high-profile case was not only a necessary political act, but one that came quite naturally to him. When he wasn't the sheriff of Eddy County, he was known as the Singing Sheriff of Eddy County, the front man in a local country-western band that played every Friday night at the Quality Inn.

"What did you say your name was?" the reporters asked him on the phone.

"Chunky," he'd respond. "M. A. Chunky Click."

The sheriff was a man blessed with an eternal shell of baby fat, from the raspberry pads of his cheeks down to his gunny-sack belly. The "M. A." stood for Mark Anthony, but in high school his friends had dubbed him Chunky, and for obvious reasons the nickname stuck. More accurately, he had embraced it.

In a state where the office of sheriff has a rich and colorful history, Carlsbad has a few tales of its own, beginning with the very first sheriff, Dave Kemp, who in 1897 gunned down his successor and bitter rival, Les Dow, in front of the Argus newspaper building on Fox Street. (Kemp, who was later referred to in a newspaper story as a "Texas killer, range rustler, and gambler" allegedly paid off a witness to say Dow had drawn first.) By the time Chunky Click took office in 1996, the days of flamboyant lawmen had long passed, consigned to history and Hollywood, but he had brought some drama back to the office when he wound up in what was hailed as a twentieth-century showdown between sheriffs.

Before Click was sheriff, he was a deputy, and in 1995 he decided to run against his boss, sitting sheriff Jack Childress. Everything was calm until four months before the Democratic primary, when Click found himself facing allegations of evidence theft in what he said was a smear campaign cooked up by Childress. Three years earlier, he had confiscated a .380-caliber Lorcin pistol from a Carlsbad youth and never returned it. Click claimed the boy's mother had asked him to hold on to it until his eighteenth birthday and that, in the meantime, he'd lent it to a friend. Despite the mudslinging, Click won the primary by a narrow 199 votes. But four months after he took office, a grand jury went ahead and indicted him on nine counts, including two for evidence tampering.

The legal shootout made state headlines. If Click was convicted, Childress would undoubtedly win back the star. Click hired Gary Mitchell, a well-known criminal defense attorney up in Ruidoso. Mitchell spent most of his time crusading against capital punishment, arguing death penalty cases, appealing sentences, and racking up a record of legal victories that at the time was approaching 100–0. Click figured if Mitchell's courtroom wizardry had saved all those men from lethal injection, he would have no problem keeping a sheriff facing politically inspired charges out of jail. He was right. After a weeklong trial, the jury found him not guilty of evidence theft, deadlocked on the remaining eight counts, and the case was dropped. Chunky Click got to keep his star, and he won a new role for himself—the underdog. At the time of the Rattlesnake Canyon killing, he had a year left on his term and was planning to run for reelection.

Click hadn't been able to tell the reporters much about the Kodikian case. But with all the attention, he was eager for new information, so when Carrasco and Ballard returned from the canyon with the evidence bags, he let his phone ring and joined them in Carrasco's office to get an update.

In addition to the journal, and the trove of items they had listed on the warrant, Carrasco and Ballard had found several other curious pieces of evidence. They had noticed that next to the campsite were the ashen remains of two fires. One was much larger than the other, and in it they found scorched pieces of green cloth and zipper teeth—apparently the remnants of a sleeping bag. Among the scattered items lying around the site they had also found food, including a plastic bag with hot-dog buns and, even more surprising, a family-size can of beans sitting unopened on a

nearby rock. Inside one of the backpacks were also numerous cactus fruits, apparently cut from the plants in the canyon. They had
found no water at the campsite, only four empty containers; three
pint bottles of White Rock water, and an empty thirty-two-ounce
container of Gatorade.

Traces of blood had been visible on a surprising number of
items. There were drops on over a dozen rocks, and streaks on
both blue foam sleeping pads and several items of clothing. All
those items, and many more, would be sent to the crime lab in
Albuquerque to be examined for DNA and trace evidence.

Jim Ballard made copies of the journal, and the four men sat
down to read and discuss it together, like members of a book club.

"Well, what do you think?" Click asked when they were all
finished.

"It sounds like these boys had it pretty rough," Carrasco
offered. No water, circling buzzards, treks to nowhere, final
farewells, a mercy killing. Jim Ballard agreed; it sounded as if they
had been through a hell of a time.

Gary McCandless thought it sounded bad, too, but was it
enough to stab your best friend in the heart? It struck him as a particularly violent and aggressive way to usher a man to his death.
Most people wouldn't have had the will to do that to an enemy,
much less a friend. He wasn't sure what to make of it. He turned to
Sheriff Click.

"What do you think?"

Click's eyes narrowed.

"Bullshit."

"What makes you think that?"

"Well, for starters, his friend never writes that he's asking

Kodikian to kill him," said the sheriff. "I mean, wouldn't he have at least done *that?*"

The other men were intrigued. It seemed like a reasonable question, given the gravity of Coughlin's alleged request. After all the explaining and good-byes he had written, why not a last note to absolve Kodikian of blame? Coughlin had to have known that even if they both died, people would figure everything out and still be uncomfortable with the image of Raffi as the merciful executioner. It was a hell of a burden to leave on a friend's shoulders without an indemnifying word. One obvious answer was that he had been too weak, or in too much pain to write or even care by then. The other obvious answer was that Coughlin hadn't written anything because he had never asked to be killed.

Either way, it quickly dawned on the four men that "he turned to me & begged that I put my knife through his chest" were the only the words indicating Coughlin's death had actually been a mercy killing, and they had been written by the killer himself, a survivor who had been able to walk out of the hospital just a little more than an hour after being admitted.

There was no way they were going to take Kodikian's story at face value.

11

David Coughlin was gone. But his body, well preserved by the dry desert air and Raffi's improvised burial cairn, still had a story to tell.

It arrived in Albuquerque late Monday night, carefully sealed in a bag with a label attached that read, "State of New Mexico, Office of the Chief Medical Investigator." In his report, Dr. Dennis Klein of the OMI would refer to the corpse as "the body"; Jim Estrada, the detective the Eddy County Sheriff's Office had assigned to witness the procedure, used "Mr. Coughlin."

When Klein unzipped the body bag, the first thing both men noticed was what appeared to be—despite the apparent hardships he had endured—a fit and healthy all-American young man. He measured Dave as just over six feet tall, his weight at 178 pounds, and noted that his overall frame was well nourished and well developed. Estrada couldn't help thinking that here was a man whose life had ended smack in its prime.

His face and chest were still covered by the blue plaid shirt, which Klein removed. Dave's eyes were fixed open, while his mouth lay closed and expressionless, set in a face flushed red with postmortem lividity. On his left breast, just to the left of his nipple, were what appeared to be two stab wounds, each about an inch long.

After Klein carefully removed Coughlin's clothes, Estrada went through the pockets of his shorts and found a wallet, four keys, some gas station receipts, and $48 in cash—nothing unexpected. He also noticed that inside his briefs was a collection of small pebbles, which he presumed had fallen in when the body was removed from the shallow grave.

Now that Dave's body was fully exposed, they began to study it closely, searching the marbled terrain of his skin for any markings—in addition to the stab wounds—that would tell a story. There were many.

Almost every surface of his skin showed some rumor of an abrasive encounter. Just above his right eyebrow was a red scrape, about half an inch square, while the back of his head bore a 2 x 2-inch bruise. His arms and legs were similarly covered with small cuts and bruises. The detective observed as Klein dictated the injuries into a mini–cassette recorder.

"What do you think of these scratches?" Estrada asked, pointing to Coughlin's shins. Both bore numerous vertical cuts that were about seven inches long. Some appeared to be scabbed over; others were fresh.

"Could be a result of vegetation," Klein said. For a second opinion, he called over Dr. Jerri McLemore, the senior medical investigator on duty, who concurred.

"Is it possible that they came from running through the vegetation, or stepping down on it?" Estrada asked. McLemore knew what he was getting at. Could the scratches indicate that Coughlin had possibly been fleeing from an attacker?

"It's possible," McLemore said, "but without any more information to go on it's just a theory."

When they turned up Coughlin's right wrist, they saw three parallel cuts, neatly horizontal, typical of a suicide attempt. But if David Coughlin had tried to kill himself, it appeared he had not tried very hard. They did not even penetrate the skin.

In all, they counted a total of nineteen blunt force injuries, but except for the cuts on Coughlin's wrists neither Klein nor McLemore could say whether they had been inflicted by a person, or the rugged canyon terrain.

Estrada photographed the body, then Klein used a large scalpel to make the classic Y-shaped incision from Coughlin's shoulders to his pelvis, careful to avoid disturbing the stab wounds. As the internal examination got under way, they saw that both wounds had completely penetrated Coughlin's chest, and that one of them had grazed a rib on the way in. Just how deep the wound tracks had gone was evident moments later after Klein removed the breast plate: Coughlin's pericardium, a thin, normally pink-colored membrane that surrounds the heart, was dark and inflamed with blood. David Coughlin, it appeared, had died from two stab wounds to the heart.

Although the stab wounds were the obvious players in Coughlin's death, there were other, more molecular tales locked inside his body. Klein removed Coughlin's heart and his other major organs, all of which he weighed, measured, and, in some cases, drained of their fluids so that their chemical contents could be analyzed later. When Klein removed Coughlin's spleen, he found that it contained 105 milliliters of urine—an indication that his kidneys, often the first organ to fail in a dehydration victim, were still functioning when he was killed. There was also a small, bright green mass of fecal matter in his bowel that appeared vegetable in origin.

Klein submitted his final report two days later, listing "stab wounds to the chest" as the cause of the death. Based on the chemical work, which showed that Coughlin had heightened levels of sodium, potassium, nitrogen, glucose, and creatinine in his blood, Klein's official assessment was that Coughlin was "moderately to severely" dehydrated at the time of his death, but "very much alive."

It was his opinion that if Raffi Kodikian hadn't stabbed him, David Coughlin almost certainly would have lived.

———

Raffi's father, Hal Kodikian, had thought his son was joking on Sunday night when he'd called from the medical center and told him the tragic news. Like the Coughlins, he and his wife, Doris, hadn't heard from Raffi since New Orleans, and had simply assumed that he and Dave were too busy having fun to bother calling home. When the gravity in his son's voice convinced him that it was true—David was dead and Raffi was about to be arrested for murder—he and Doris found themselves in a nightmare of grief, fear, and incomprehension second only that of Bob and Joyce Coughlin.

Hal immediately booked a flight for New Mexico and arrived in Carlsbad Monday evening after a sleepless night and an anxious, lonely plane flight across the country. He was nearly heart-broken when he arrived in Carlsbad and was told that visiting hours at the jail weren't until Friday, and infinitely grateful when he was given special permission to see Raffi that night. As he waited in the visiting room behind a Plexiglas window, the anticipation of finally seeing his son was crushing. When a guard brought Raffi in, tears of happiness pooled in his eyes despite the horrible circumstances.

"When [you see your son in jail] the first thing you look at is what he looks like," he later said, "and he looked fine. He looked all right, and that made me feel a lot better."

Hal had a thousand questions for his son. He and his wife were as confounded by Raffi's story as anyone else. Later he would acknowledge that his son's story was "bizarre," but when he picked up the phone and spoke, he didn't press Raffi for hard details. He and Doris were convinced from the beginning that their boy had done exactly what they had raised him to do: he had told the truth.

I'm trying to find you a lawyer, he told Raffi. I'm going to do everything I can to get you out of jail.

The next morning, he did just that. He had $50,000 wired to a bank in Carlsbad, converted it into a cashier's check, and immediately posted bail at the courthouse. Judge Lyons, who was accustomed to setting bail for people who had far more difficulty coming up with much less money, was stunned. Most of the time, the only way a defendant could pay a $50,000 cash bond was to enlist the services of bondsman, who might charge ten times that if a client skipped bail. Technically, it had been one of the highest bails he had ever set, but by Tuesday afternoon, Raffi was free to go.

The task of bailing out his son had distracted Hal from his grief, but when there was nothing left to do but wait while the jail processed Raffi for release, he fell apart.

"He was sitting in a chair outside my office, and he just looked like he was about to die," Gary McCandless remembered of Hal. "He couldn't understand what had happened to his son, and he felt horrible for the Coughlins. I've met a lot of people in my business, and if there's one thing I learned about Hal Kodikian it was that he is a good man. A *good* man."

McCandless, a father himself, felt awful for Hal. He knew it was going to be a long week ahead for the father; according to Raffi's bail limitations, he couldn't leave the county, and the Kodikians knew no one in Carlsbad and nothing about the town. As Hal wiped away his tears and prepared to leave with his son, the detective offered to give them a tour, and Hal took him up on it.

"I showed them where the best restaurants were, the movie theater, and the banks," McCandless said. "Raffi didn't say much. He was pretty quiet. He sat in the backseat."

That was no surprise, given that his dad was riding shotgun with the man investigating him for murder. For much of the next week, Raffi would remain quiet, avoiding the reporters in town by laying low at the Quality Inn, where he and his father took a room under an assumed name. It was a lonesome hideaway, clinging to the edge of town out on Highway 62/180, the nothingness of the desert just beyond its marquee. Even in an air-conditioned room, he could feel the desert's presence right outside, hear its vacuity in the long howls of semis as they passed down the same road that he and Dave had taken only a week earlier.

He didn't blame himself for Dave's death—in his mind he had

had no other choice—but if statements he would later make were true, he did feel as if his own survival was a crime. All he could think about was Dave's family, two thousand miles away, on their knees in the basement of sorrow. More than anything, he wanted to talk to the Coughlins, to tell them in his own words what had happened.

Hal did his best to comfort his son, but he was hurting himself. He dropped by the sheriff's office almost every day just to check in with Gary McCandless. It was a gesture a lawman in a county less than a hundred miles from the sanctuary of the Mexican border could appreciate, but there was more to it than that. In what would be one of the oddest relationships born from the case, Hal Kodikian and Gary McCandless became friends.

"We talked about family, about raising children, about life," McCandless recalled. "We didn't talk much about the case. I told him up front that it was my job to make sure every question about the killing was answered, and he respected that."

Despite the detective's genuine sympathy and affection for Hal, he had serious questions about Raffi's story. Even while Hal sat in his office, drinking coffee and rubbing the tears out of his eyes, McCandless had to explain—as gingerly as he could—that he was going to need blood, saliva, and handwriting samples from his son. Every cold, clinical detail—no matter how gingerly the detective put it—just drove home the awful reality for Hal. McCandless tried to comfort him by explaining that the evidence could indeed support his son's story, but also warned him that—even if it did—his son would still need a strong attorney in his corner.

McCandless, in fact, had an attorney in mind, but he didn't think it was his place to recommend him. He was relieved on

Wednesday when Hal dropped by to tell him he had found one. Three different lawyers back East had all given him the same name: Gary Mitchell, from Ruidoso, the very lawyer McCandless would have suggested.

"Well, you're in good hands," the detective told Hal. He couldn't help being tickled by the irony: Mitchell was not only the same attorney who had defended Sheriff Click during the evidence-tampering debacle, but his own lawyer as well.

12

There's a small statuette that can be found in almost every tourist shop in New Mexico. It's an image of a cowboy—a broncobuster—riding wildly on the back of a bucking horse. Whether it's done in pewter, bronze, or carved out of imported mahogany, the cowboy is especially long and wiry, a creature of motion and hunger who bends his back in impossible arches and is somehow both rugged and wispily adaptable at the same time. He is the gaunt trickster of the plains, undefeatable, forever on the verge of a fall that never comes.

At a lanky six feet three and a half inches, Gary Mitchell could have served as a model for those statues. It was much easier to picture him on the back of a bronco than it was to envision him in front of the state supreme court, his steel blue eyes softened by a sincerity in his voice as he pleaded to keep the most cold-blooded criminals in the state off death row. Child murderers, cop killers, and Ricky Abeyta, the state's biggest mass murderer in modern history, were among the nearly one hundred men he had represented since New Mexico reinstated the death penalty in 1978. Some got life in prison, some were acquitted, but not one of his clients had ever felt the needle of lethal injection. And if there were indeed analogies between breaking wild horses and coaxing New Mexico juries to show mercy toward men who possessed none themselves, Mitchell was the man to make them. When he wasn't in court, he could usually be found working at some corner of his father-in-law's ten-section cattle ranch in a pair of Wranglers and boots, which was also what he wore to the office.

"I'd be perfectly happy as a rancher," he was fond of telling the reporters who followed his cases, "but there's God's work to be done, and I was raised to believe that an eye for an eye makes the whole world blind."

That Mitchell actually *was* a cowboy had a great deal to do with his success. In the early days, district attorneys had snickered when he drove to trials in a king cab pickup and walked in wearing a western-cut suit, but they soon learned to respect him. In New Mexico cowboying is still the most honest work a man can do, and jurors could spy the cowboy in Gary Mitchell a mile away. They listened raptly to his arguments for that very reason: he wasn't a liberal city slicker educated at an East Coast college; he was their own Atticus Finch, raised on a farm outside of Santa Fe, and he knew what it was to make a living with his hands. His own father had been killed in a tractor accident when he was nineteen, and whether his clients were accused of murder, petty theft, or traffic violations, he had always tried to portray the side of them that was pure working man.

Judge Lyons gave Raffi permission to leave Eddy County to visit

Mitchell, and he and his father made the three-hour drive up to Ruidoso. As they drove north to Roswell, then east, the sun-bitten land gave way to cultivated fields, which in turn gave way to the dark and crowded pine forests of the Sacramento Mountains and New Mexico high country. It was a different world, Ruidoso, a mountain playground with casinos, a horse track, and a ski resort.

Mitchell's office was a church of oak. Bookcases, paneling—all of it was natural and unfinished except for his desk, a huge and beautifully gnarled laminated crescent. On the wall behind it a large oil canvas depicted life on the range. Hal Kodikian left his son alone with the tall lawyer, and it was there, in that venerable den of rawhide and wood, that Gary Mitchell became the first person to hear Kodikian's full version of what had transpired in Rattlesnake Canyon.

"He hadn't told his father, or his mother, what had happened," Mitchell said in a light New Mexico drawl. "That just wasn't his way. He wanted to spare them the pain. You know, I've represented some evil men, but Raffi Kodikian isn't one of them. His was a case of bad luck."

As Mitchell listened to Raffi's account of his and Dave's ordeal in the canyon and the mercy killing, an old story his father once told him surfaced in memory: A man was driving down one of New Mexico's empty highways when he suddenly came upon the burning wreck of a truck. The passerby pulled over to investigate and heard screams coming from the flame-engulfed cab. There was no way the passerby could reach the trucker, and when both men realized there was no hope, the trucker yelled for the passerby to kill him before he suffered the horrible death of being cooked alive. Since New Mexico is the kind of state where it's typical for people to carry guns in their cars, the passerby ran back to his car, grabbed his rifle, and shot the trucker dead. Other cars had stopped by then, too, but when the highway patrol finally arrived, none of the onlookers said anything about the shooting.

Mitchell couldn't remember where or when the trucker incident had taken place. Maybe it never had; such legends came with the landscape. Whether it was real or not was less important to the lawyer than the idea that it could have been, and Raffi's story was a living cousin. David Coughlin had been the trucker, Kodikian the passerby, and if the case went to trial, he would have to turn the jury into the approbative onlookers.

Another story Mitchell quickly latched on to was one of oldest in the West: the tenderfoot. Mitchell was a connoisseur of western lore; he had a degree in American history and kept in his truck a well-worn copy of Paul Horgan's masterpiece *Great River: The Rio Grande in North American History*, which he dipped into between court sessions. But it didn't take an expert to see that Kodikian fit the tenderfoot profile perfectly. He had come from the East, ignorant and overconfident when it came to the power of the desert. He had neglected to bring enough water with him, failed to mark his surroundings; and sure enough, tragedy had ensued. "These boys just didn't know what they were getting into," he would later say. "Raffi wants to live and write in a Hemingway style, but he doesn't have the Hemingway ability to survive."

But cases weren't won on stories alone. They were won on the law, and in this department Mitchell knew that Raffi had a problem.

He told Raffi up front that his defense might have to somehow revolve around the idea that he wasn't in his right mind when he killed Coughlin. In other words, insanity, but as far he knew insanity had never been used in a case like his, simply because there had never been a case like his. Precedents were thin, which meant that defenses would be, too. In a worst-case scenario—a conviction— they could ask for a pardon, which he thought Raffi had a good chance of obtaining, thanks to the mitigating circumstances of their desert ordeal.

Insanity. Pardons. To Raffi, none of it sounded good.

————

Mitchell's first job was to get Kodikian permission to return home to Pennsylvania. To get the process moving, all he had to do was pick up the phone and call his good friend and former client, Chunky Click. The two men had seen each other often since Click's own trial. They lunched together whenever Mitchell breezed into Carlsbad for a court hearing, and if there was a trial, they might even end up drinking a few beers together at Click's house. Mitchell knew Click well enough to know he'd want something before he'd support allowing Kodikian to leave the county. They jawed for a few minutes, inquiring about each other's family, then he agreed to let the sheriff's investigators interview Kodikian, provided they didn't ask him any questions about what happened after the friends had arrived in the park.

The interview took place in the sheriff's office, on Friday, August 13. Kodikian, Mitchell, Eddie Carrasco, and John Andrews sat down in the conference room, and Raffi told the investigators about the road trip, naming the cities and places they'd visited, and any addresses he could remember. Carrasco then left the conference room, then Jim Ballard came in with a search warrant for an example of Kodikian's handwriting. Also present was Hal

Kodikian, who watched quietly as his son filled in the standard forms with letters of the alphabet, days of the week, names, and occupations. Afterward Ballard read from a copy of the journal and asked Raffi to transcribe. This was particularly important, because the investigators had noticed earlier that two of the journal entries were signed "David" and appeared to be in a different handwriting than the rest of the content. One was from Friday, August 4; the other from the Saturday, August 5, David Coughlin's last day of life.

"I do not know what to do right now," Ballard slowly dictated from the journal, "but I am in utter agony and I know you would understand."

Kodikian began to write, then stopped. He asked his father to leave the room, sobbed quietly for a few moments, then continued. It was the first time Kodikian showed remorse in front of the investigators. After he was finished, Ballard put the test in an envelope and mailed it to the U.S. Secret Service office in Albuquerque for handwriting analysis.

13

David Coughlin's memorial service was held on a rainy Saturday afternoon a week after the killing. It was the kind of warm, airy drizzle that comes to eastern Massachusetts during the late summer, barely a tenth of an inch, but enough to make a few of the mourners wonder.

"Dave definitely would have considered that funny," one of them later said. "I could almost hear him laughing at it, saying, 'It just figures the damn water would come *now*.'"

Only hours before the ceremony began, Judge Lyons had given Kodikian permission to return home—an unusual privilege for a man charged with murder. Most of the guests at Coughlin's funeral had not yet heard the news that his killer had been set free. Quite a few of them, in fact, had never even heard of Kodikian before the killing, and were surprised that the newspaper and television reports were referring to him as David's "best friend." It was plain enough from the turnout that Coughlin had a lot friends. More than three hundred mourners filled the pews at Saint James the Great Catholic Church, a grand and elegant brick house of worship next to Route 9 in Wellesley.

The list of speakers was long. There were people from college, people from the town hall, people from high school whom he hadn't spoken to in years. Over the past week, Kodikian's bizarre story of what happened had made Coughlin's death larger than his life; many of his friends had been unable to begin processing the pain because they didn't have a clear picture of what had happened. Many never would. But on that day, at least, they tried to put aside their astonishment and speculation and remember their friend.

Coughlin's family sat in the front pews, the eyes of the entire congregation upon them. They had come to say good-bye to their son and brother, but people were also looking to them in order to know how to be. So far, they had remained silent about their position on Kodikian's story, avoiding a merciless media assault. Outside the church, camera crews from the Boston TV stations were setting up, their lenses trained on the doors in order to make brutally public that awful, personal loss on the family's faces. Even now, reporters who had snuck in were sitting in the pews behind them, quietly taking notes, fishing for anything that would move the story forward. They would not be disappointed.

Toward the end of the ceremony, David's brother, Michael, ascended the pulpit and began an emotional remembrance of his little brother. After telling an amusing story from their childhood in which David had once refused to eat his dinner beets, he drew some merciful laughter from the crowd, then at last made the family's first public statement about the killing.

"This is very, very important to me," he said, his eyes fixed on the nave. "Everyone here, please say a prayer for Raffi, because I know how much he loved David and I know how much my brother loved him."

A heavy hush followed. How much of it was prayer, and how much of it was disbelief that Michael had expressed support for his brother's killer so soon after his death, only the mourners know, but from that moment on, it was clear where the Coughlins stood: they believed Raffi. It came down to incredible heart and faith in their son's choices, and a conscious decision not to embrace rage as a fulcrum to ease their loss. They had chosen the hardest road of all, and one that very few people at the funeral were prepared to go down at that point.

"Jaws dropped," recalled Kristen Fischer, a childhood friend who was at the ceremony and is still mystified by Michael Coughlin's words. "I mean, 'Pray for *Raffi?*' What about pray for *David?*" Fischer had grown up right up the street from Coughlin and had actually been his first crush, one of those girls he liked but had been too shy to approach. In their junior year, however, Coughlin confessed his feelings for her in a letter. She never saw it. Perhaps sensing that his affections wouldn't be returned, he crumpled it up and threw it away, but it came back to haunt him. Fischer's brother, who was friends with David's sister, Kathy, was over visiting the Coughlins and spied the discarded letter in a garbage can. Seeing his sister's name at the top, he couldn't resist fishing it out and reading it.

"It was a crush letter. It said things like, 'I really like you, I haven't been able to tell you'—the whole thing. And my brother just opened it up and pulled it out and read the whole thing in front of all his high-school friends. And they're laughing away, putting their feet up and joking, and David came in. My brother told me that his face just got bright red, then he grabbed the letter and left. He didn't say a word."

Coughlin's contained reaction to what must have been one of his life's most embarrassing moments, Fischer said, was indicative of his personality as a whole. She believes he would have faced his ordeal in the canyon with calmness and determination, and, more important, wouldn't have placed his friend in the position of being the vehicle of his death.

"I could see him jumping off a cliff before he asked his best friend to put a knife in his heart," she said. "Even if Raffi had it in him to kill him, I could see David not wanting to bother somebody else or hurt somebody else, or bring somebody else into his pain and his world of trauma and trial and tribulation. I could not see him dragging somebody else into his problems."

———

David Coughlin had always admired the local police officers. As a kid, his favorite game was cops and robbers, and his two best friends were both sons of Wellesley cops; as a man, he had several friends who were cops themselves. Like him, most of them were local boys of Irish descent who went to the same bars he did after a day of working for the town. He'd joke with them about being the desk jockey stuck with fielding the complaints about the same parking laws they were enforcing, and they considered him one of their own. When word of his strange death went through Wellesley PD, they were not about to sit around and wait for the feds to figure out if there was another reason Raffi might have wanted to kill Dave. They were going to look into it themselves.

Terrence Cunningham, the deputy chief of police, immediately started his own investigation. Cunningham had known Coughlin most of the time he had worked for the town, and had always liked his attitude. The defeatist vision of Coughlin giving up and begging to be killed was unacceptable to the deputy chief. From Cunningham's experience, Dave Coughlin was anything but a quitter. He was animated and full of life, and he accomplished his goals. He ran in the local charity races the department threw, and in the months before he left, Coughlin had been attending the gym religiously, building up his muscle mass. The idea that he had physically caved while Kodikian had hung on seemed far-fetched.

Cunningham set up a meeting with two younger men who he knew were close to Dave: Chris Clark, a coworker at the town hall, and one of his own police officers, Terrance Connelly. Connelly, he knew, was fired up about the killing, eager to help. He was one of Coughlin's best friends, and whenever Dave had dropped by the station on a social visit, it was usually to meet up with him. Also present was Dave's boss, Arnold Wakelin, and Ernest Gagnon, Wellesley's chief of police.

You guys know any another reason why this guy might have wanted to kill Dave? he asked the two men.

Clark couldn't think of anything, but Connelly immediately thought of Kirsten Swan. He knew that she was Raffi's ex-girlfriend, and that Dave had known her first and had always been close to her. He also knew that she had gone with him to California back in May. Perhaps they had been closer than Kodikian liked.

What exactly are we talking about? How close? Cunningham asked.

Connelly's next words would be recorded in the deputy chief's police report, which he later submitted to both the FBI and the Eddy County Sheriff's Office: "Mr. Connelly informed me that on one occasion that David told him that he had been intimate with Swan," read the report.

For an investigator looking for a motive other than mercy, Connelly's statement was a good place to start.

————

Finding out if there was any truth to the doubts people had about Raffi's story fell on Larry Travaglia, a thirty-six-year-old special agent with the FBI. A native of Huntington, Long Island, he seemed as East as Chunky Click was West. He looked like Robert De Niro, spoke with an East Coast assonance, and had five cousins and an uncle in the NYPD. He would have gone to work for the NYPD, too, but at the time he decided to go into law enforcement they weren't offering the test. He had gone into the FBI instead, and had been with the bureau's Violent Crimes Task Force in Boston since 1990. He'd worked on several high-profile investigations, including the Unabomber and Timothy McVeigh cases, but nothing in his experience prepared him for his first visit to the Coughlin house, two days after the memorial service.

"It was looking into David's father's eyes and his mother's eyes and having them, you know, hysterically crying and talking about their love for their child and now their child is gone," he remembered. "It's something that's gonna stick with you for a while."

What also stuck with him was their readiness to believe and forgive Kodikian.

"Mr. Coughlin said to the effect, 'If Raffi killed my son, there had to be a good reason for it, and I hold no malice toward him,' " Travaglia recalled. He was stunned. "I just don't know how they could make that determination without really knowing all of the facts. I mean, this was relatively soon after the incident that they were basically proclaiming Raffi's innocence. It's a testament to what type of people they are, though, that they would be willing to forgive somebody for what he had done to their son."

Not everyone was so trusting, or forgiving, of Kodikian. Wellesley deputy chief Cunningham set up an interview between Special Agent Travaglia and Terry Connelly, the local police officer who Cunningham had written up in his report as having said that Coughlin had once "been intimate" with Kirsten Swan. According to Travaglia, during the interview, Connelly again "alluded to the fact that he felt something was going on" between Coughlin and Swan, but this time he wouldn't go into specifics. Travaglia left the interview disappointed, but still hopeful. With the Coughlin family more or less supporting Kodikian's story, it was understandable if Connelly had second thoughts about introducing an alternate theory that might not be corroborated.

Deputy Chief Cunningham was less understanding.

"After the interview, I spoke with Connelly and asked him why he did not tell SA Travaglia what he had previously stated to me regarding the fact that Swan and Coughlin had at some point been intimate," Cunningham wrote in his own report. "Connelly then told me that I must have misunderstood what he said to me and he stated that he did not know anything about an intimate relationship between Swan and Coughlin. I reminded him that

Mr. Wakelin, Mr. Clark, and Chief Gagnon were all present when he made those remarks. He again stated that either he misunderstood the question or I misunderstood his response."

Travaglia was hopeful that, if Connelly's August 9 statement was true, other friends of Coughlin would know about it. On August 17, he interviewed Keith Goddard, Coughlin's former roommate, who lived in the apartment he and Coughlin had shared in Millis. He told Travaglia that he, too, suspected something had been going on between Coughlin and Swan, but had no definite knowledge of a tryst. If Coughlin had been secretly attracted to her, he kept it to himself. Despite Coughlin's closeness to her, Goddard never met her until Coughlin's funeral.

Like everyone else who knew Coughlin, Goddard was devastated, and having trouble picturing Coughlin begging to be killed. As roommates and friends, he and Coughlin had occasionally stayed up late chatting, sharing their ideas about life. Since Coughlin's death, one of those conversations had kept haunting him. They had been discussing death itself, and at one point Goddard had said that he would rather die before any of his family members. Coughlin had adamantly taken the opposite view, and couldn't understand how Goddard could want such a thing. "Think about your mother," he had said. Over the years Goddard had known him, Dave had never once mentioned feeling suicidal. "I never saw an individual as happy as Coughlin," he told Travaglia, "which is one of the reasons why I liked associating with him."

The only thing that did jibe with Goddard was the image of Coughlin having a hard time in the wilderness. He and Coughlin had once gone on a river-rafting trip, and he remembered

Coughlin struggling and, at one point, losing patience with the rigors of the outdoors. Even so, he told Travaglia that "Coughlin was an optimist who would have toughed it out until the rangers arrived."

Sonnet Frost, Coughlin's girlfriend, used the exact same words, describing David as "a guy who would tough it out." Frost had a hard time believing Kodikian's story about a mercy killing, and when Travaglia showed her a copy of the journal she found Coughlin's entries curious. They appeared to be in his handwriting, but some of the things he said didn't fit with the man she knew. "We had forever but now all we have is eternity," he wrote to her at one point. "You will always be in my heart and you will always have an angel standing by."

"David was not religious," she told Travaglia. "He didn't believe in angels, and he didn't believe in an afterlife."

Goddard had also said the same thing. Although Coughlin dutifully went to church and Sunday school throughout his childhood, after he left home for college he began to develop his own views about religion. Whether it was the sort of classic and temporary rebellion from the religion forced on him since childhood, or a permanent shift in his spirituality, his closest friends knew him not only as nonreligious, but as an atheist. The only explanations for the religious references Frost could think of were that the entries were simply false, or written with the idea of soothing his parents, who would have wanted him to find God. Faced with an agonizing plight in Rattlesnake Canyon, he may have done just that.

Like Goddard, Frost didn't know about any affair between her boyfriend and Swan. If she had her suspicions, she kept them to herself and wasn't able to offer Travaglia any other reason why Kodikian might want to kill Coughlin. Travaglia decided it was time to question Swan herself.

Kirsten Swan hadn't known the full details of David's death. All she knew was that Dave was dead, Raffi had been arrested, and there was nebulous talk about mercy killing and suicide. She did not believe that Raffi had actually killed Dave. When Travaglia went over to her apartment in Boston to interview her, he found himself in the added position as the bearer of bad news.

"I unfortunately had to tell her that it looked like a murder," Travaglia said. "Because she didn't know. She just simply knew that David had been killed, and wasn't really sure of the circumstances, and I had to inform her that her boyfriend killed her friend."

Swan was understandably shocked, and Travaglia avoided pressing further on the nature of her relationship with Coughlin. She told him that David was a friend, and that she knew of no animosity between him and Raffi. But by the time he had his second interview with her, he had a police report from Terry Cunningham detailing Connelly's statement about David "having been intimate with her on occasion" and this time he confronted her directly, asking her about the trip to California and if she and David had been more than friends. Her demeanor, said the investigator, changed immediately.

"When I started to propose some speculative theories as to a possible murder motive as to why this thing transpired, the interview went right away from being cooperative to somewhat defensive," Travaglia said. Before answering any more questions, Swan said she wanted to speak to her lawyer.

Travaglia was once again disappointed, but he understood Swan's reaction as a natural one. She was as surprised as anyone else at the killing, and had no way of knowing whether her relationship with Coughlin—especially if it *had* been more than a friendship—was the actual motive. To admit to having had a sexual encounter with Coughlin would have put her in a position even more conflicted than Connelly's. She could be called as a witness for the prosecution, quite probably a hostile one, and end up admitting to a tryst that could very well provide a skeptical jury with exactly what it needed to fill in the blanks and put Kodikian away for good. Before crossing that Rubicon, she had to be sure exactly which side of it she stood on.

Travaglia also interviewed Kodikian's coworkers at Massachusetts Financial Services, and found that none of them had any reason to believe Kodikian might have been lying about the mercy killing.

"There was really nothing to indicate that there was an issue with temper or anything like that," said the agent. "Nothing in the personality makeup whatsoever to indicate that he would be capable of such an act. There might have been a slight reference that one individual saw him blow up one time, but it was like a one-time quick shot with really nothing to it. And his girlfriend never alluded to the fact that he had any type of mean streak or temper. The Coughlin family spoke very highly of him. We didn't come across one person that said, 'Whoa. That guy had a temper that you really gotta watch out for.' "

14

Once a month, a program on a computer at the Eddy County Courthouse randomly decides which of the county's seven prosecutors will be on call each weekend. The process—like so many rituals of the justice system—is meant to ensure fairness and impartiality. So it was that a mathematical algorithm brought Lesley Williams the strangest case of his career.

Les Williams was about as far from a big-city prosecutor as one could get. Opening the door to his office a month after Kodikian's arrest, he immediately made it clear that he was keeping his cards to himself until the trial. "C'mon in, have a seat. . . . But I warn you, I'm not going to talk about the case," were the first words he said.

Unlike Gary Mitchell, who could effortlessly jaw a reporter into a state of pleasant oblivion and leave him no hard answers, Les seemed guarded and uncomfortable around the media. He had the slim, angular build of a preacher, and he'd cross his long arms in front of his chest protectively, quickly warning reporters when they were heading down a road that might get him in trouble. Often he'd answer a question with a yes or a no and a smile, indicating he clearly knew they had hoped for a more elaborate response. He would not let slip a single opinion or tidbit about the investigation, not even a quiver of prosecutorial passion.

But he was certainly passionate about Carlsbad, and he offered to give a tour of the town. The first stop was Carlsbad's historical centerpiece, an old viaduct built in 1902 that locals simply called the Flume. Fed by a raised canal from a reservoir upriver, it allowed the captured water of the Pecos actually to cross over itself and irrigate over twenty thousand acres of vital farmland east of the town. He walked down to the river's cool edge and stood under the Flume's wide cement arches. It was an impressive feat of engineering, one that had been featured on *Ripley's Believe It or Not.*

"This is it," Les said, looking up at the arches with his hands plugged into his pockets. "It's not the Great Wall of China, but this is what makes it all happen."

He explained that the original flume had been build of wood but had washed away in the flood of 1893. It had been part of Charles Eddy and Pat Garrett's vast irrigation project, which ultimately turned out to be an expensive lesson in the dangers of water gambling. In front of him the Pecos flowed peacefully, a light breeze licking facets onto its surface and rustling the cattails on its shore. But it had a capricious temperament. It had flooded a dozen times in the town's history, and just as often the desert had squeezed it into a trickle, bringing the farms and cattle ranches to the brink of annihilation.

Fifty yards downriver was what looked like a shorefront ruin: a series of square, algae-lined cement tanks, open to the sky and set back from the river. A decadent, sulfurous wisp in the air betrayed the presence of a mineral spring. Was it the ruin of an old wash tank, or a flooded building foundation? It was impossible to tell.

"Oh, *that*," he said with a sardonic grin. "That's the spa."

The spa had been Plan B, the very source of the town's name. It was one of the Southwest's first attempts at marketing itself as a retirement community, but it was clearly ahead of its time. Few could make the illustrious European connection, and most of those who did knew a smelly gurgle in the middle of a sun-stricken territory when they saw one.

Williams's next stop was the highest point in the area, a five-hundred-foot-high hill on the west side of town. Toward the summit, the houses grew in size, and at the crest were lawny and elaborate pueblo-style spreads with spotless adobe walls and two-car garages. In the suburb of a large city, the houses would have never stood out, but here they were mansions. Who lived in them?

"Mostly people who work for the WIPP," Les said without a beat, referring to what is now the town's main industry, the Waste Isolation Pilot Plant, which proudly claims the title of being "the world's first underground repository licensed to safely and permanently dispose of transuranic radioactive waste left from the research and production of nuclear weapons." Few towns had wanted to host the project, but Carlsbad had lobbied hard for it, and it had brought hundreds of jobs and millions in government revenue. It had begun operations just that March, and not even Les could help marveling at Carlsbad's nouveauo richeo, the nuclear-waste barons, high on their hill. "There used to be nothing up here," he said. "We used to drive up here and park when we were kids."

Inspiration Point?

"Something like that."

Below was the whole town, brushed into life by the river's water and motionless in the heat except for the occasional spear of sunlight on car metal. Beyond the river's reach the desert lay endless and empty, a giant piecrust that seemed poised to color the little city brown at any moment. It had nearly done so several times, and one can't help thinking that Carlsbad's greatest bulwark against civic evaporation lies not in the flow of the Pecos, but in the stubbornness and tenacity of the townspeople. One gets the impression that, if the river turned to dust tomorrow, instead of leaving they'd simply devise a way to sell sand.

Only two things had ever dragged Les away: college and the Vietnam War. In college, he had joined a work-abroad program that sent him to the Philippines and Greenland, and after getting his bachelor's degree he enlisted in the navy. Aboard a guided missile cruiser, he saw action on the gun line off North Vietnam. After his tour of duty, he entered law school at the University of New Mexico, but almost as soon as he passed the bar the navy recalled him. They sent him to Pearl Harbor, where he spent three years in the Naval Legal Service Office. By the time he was honorably discharged, Les had seen more of the world than he ever imagined, and he was certain where he belonged. He made a beeline straight back to Carlsbad.

His first job was at the district attorney's office, where he worked for five years, became head of the office, then left to try his hand at private practice. He practiced general law, doing everything from divorces to torts and even some criminal cases. There were two rules he always followed. He told his clients point-blank that if they were guilty then he would not represent them unless they actually *pled* guilty, and he also warned them that if he found out they were lying, then they would have to find another lawyer. He had only been lied to one time, by a client charged with the inglorious crime of "scouting"—using bait in a deer hunt. Luckily, the man's wife had called him the day before the trial and confessed that her husband was guilty as sin.

After a few years in private practice, he concluded "that most people were more interested in using lawyers to help them get away with things than actually honoring the law and the truth." He went back to working for the district attorney with the same certainty of place that had brought him back to Carlsbad.

Les wasn't prone to fancy legal maneuvering, storytelling, or stepping out beyond what he knew to be true. It was a conservative approach, reflective of his faith that if he stuck to the facts, true justice would—or at least should—follow. His gift was for cutting through the smokescreens that defense lawyers threw up, for simplifying a case to its indisputable golden core. And, as for the core of the Kodikian case, if the murder investigation found an alternative motive, fine; if not, there was still one thing he knew, and when he pointed it out, he did so with great conviction.

"You don't get to kill someone in the state of New Mexico just because they ask you to," he said. "That is the law."

The only other case of his that had received so much media attention had been a death penalty case he and the district attorney, Tom Rutledge, had tried against Terry Clark, a man from the nearby town of Artesia who had kidnapped, raped, and then murdered a nine-year-old girl. The case had gone on for thirteen years, reappearing in the news like a season. Clark had appealed the sentence twice, lost both times, and ended up being the first man executed in the state in forty years. Les didn't like to talk much about that case, either, but there was a little-known detail about the Terry Clark case that Raffi Kodikian and his family were probably better off not knowing.

Terry Clark was the 1 in Gary Mitchell's 100–1 record of death penalty cases. Les Williams and Tom Rutledge were the only prosecutors in the state who had beaten the broncobuster at his own game.

15

If you look at a good map of New Mexico long enough, you begin to see that the names of certain places aren't really names at all, but stories. No Agua. Dead Man's Lake. Dead Horse Gulch, Skeleton Canyon. They tell of inglorious battles against a rugged landscape that were lost long ago.

It's impossible to know just how many souls have been lost in the desert of southern New Mexico over the ages; like the sea, the desert is good at keeping its victims' secrets. There are, however, several legendary episodes that provide an idea of the scale of suffering the desert is capable of wreaking on those who enter it without enough water.

One occurred in September 1681, an age in which the history of the American West was written by Spain. That summer, the local Pueblo Indians had violently rebelled against their Spanish colonizers, driving them out of Santa Fe and northern New Mexico in what later came to be known as the Pueblo Revolt. The survivors of the uprising, about twenty-five hundred Spanish men, women, and children, fled south and gathered at Fray Cristobal, a waypoint about halfway between Santa Fe and El Paso, a few miles from what is today the White Sands Missile Range. They were refugees, with no other option but to retreat farther south to the protection at El Paso. Between them and their destination lay the same ninety miles of flat and completely waterless desert that the founders of Santa Fe had called el Jornada del Muerto, "the journey of the dead."

What ensued was one of the worst human disasters that ever befell colonists in North America. The crossing began on September 14, with the refugees marching toward the Jornada in what was already a sorry-looking column. Several witnesses who saw the group just prior to their departure described it as mostly barefoot women and children, with no more water than they could carry in small containers and only enough food for two days. The lack of adequate supplies was considered a temporary problem, however, because the column was expecting to be met early on by twenty-four wagons with relief provisions sent from El Paso. So they sallied forth into the dunes and yucca, unaware that the rescue wagons had not even left yet.

No eyewitness accounts of the passage remain, but dark math tells part of the story. It takes nine days to cross the Jornada on foot, which would have left the party without food—and probably almost no water—two or three days into their trek, about twenty miles from the nearest aid. The only hope for survival was in the promised wagon train; as the situation deteriorated, their eyes would have been trained ahead, futilely searching for the convecting shape of a horseman on the horizon. The dying would have begun very quickly, with the healthiest of them forced to witness the rapid demise of their children and elderly as they fell from heat-stroke and heat exhaustion. "A disorganized multitude of families, of exhausted, stricken mothers, of haggard fathers staggering along with dying babies in their arms, of children sobbing piteously for food and water, of a lengthening line of new graves," is how the historian Cleve Hallenbeck pictured it.

There is almost no shade in the *Jornada;* stopping to rest only meant that it would take longer to meet the supply train. As the weak fell behind and families tarried to attend to their loved ones, the line of refugees would have extended for miles, with the dazed walking past the dead and wondering how long it would be before the corpse on the side of the trail was their own. Nightfall meant temporary relief from the heat, but with an average low in mid-September of fifty-two degrees, many would have been shiv-ering, their water-deprived blood thickened and unable to warm them.

Somewhere near the southern end of the *Jornada,* the overdue wagon train and its precious barrels of water finally appeared. The weary, half-dead refugees limped into El Paso, their number dimin-ished by nearly six hundred. As Hallenbeck grimly notes: "It meant fifty or more deaths per day, or a new grave every one thou-sand feet."

In 1862 New Mexico's desert surprised yet another group of newcomers, this time Confederate Americans, an army of rebels with dreams of conquering themselves an empire that stretched all the way to the Pacific. They were led by an overweening brigadier general named Henry Sibley, and in May 1861, they crossed the Rio Grande, twenty-five hundred strong. The campaign came to a halt ten months later, and they never got farther than Albu-querque. During the battle of Glorieta Pass, a Union cavalry brigade snuck around to their rear and annihilated their supply train, effectively forcing them to fall back to Texas or starve. Like the Spanish, they were forced to retreat into the desert, and their trip back to Texas became one of the most hellish marches of the Civil War.

The retreat began in mid-April with the main body of Sibley's Brigade heading south out of Albuquerque along the Rio Grande, shadowed by a Union army under the command of Col. Edward Canby. Sibley's immediate goal was Fort Bliss, three hundred miles downriver. Following the river all the way to the fort was risky, however, because the route would take him right past the Union stronghold of Fort Craig. He chose to avoid the fort by swerving west, into the arid Magdalena Mountains, then sneaking back out onto the river below Craig. When the rebel column snaked off toward the waterless mountains, Canby made no attempt to fol-low. He knew that the rebels were about to confront an enemy far more formidable than he: the high desert.

As the column entered the range, lugging their cannons and what little remained of their supplies, the retreat quickly deterio-rated into every man for himself. A Confederate private named A. B. Peticolas wrote of the nightmarish trek in his journal: "No order was observed, no company staid together, the wearied sank down upon the grass, regardless of the cold; the strong, with words of execration upon their lips, pressed feverishly and frantically on for water. Dozens fell in together and in despair gave up all hope of getting to water and stopped, built fires, and fell asleep."

Each night, some slept for good; each day was a race between what tiny water pockets the mountains offered, if pockets could be found at all. To ease their journey, they cast off everything. They buried most of their cannons. Clothes were abandoned, rifles, ammunition. They dumped everything that might slow them down until all that was left to abandon was one another, which they did. The sick and the weak were left behind to fend for themselves against the wolves. A year later, a Union captain named James "Paddy" Graydon retraced their trail:

"On passing over the route of these unfortunate men . . . I not infrequently found a piece of a gun-carriage, or part of a harness, or some piece of camp or garrison equipage, with occasionally a white, dry skeleton of a man. At some points it seemed impossible for men to have made their way."

By the time the force reached Fort Bliss, they were in such poor condition that Sibley decided to abandon New Mexico altogether and fall back to San Antonio, Texas, which meant another six hundred miles of marching, much of it through the Chihuahuan. Sibley was so disgusted by the outcome of the invasion that in his final report on the campaign he had these bitter words: "The Territory of New Mexico is not worth a quarter of the blood and treasure expended it its conquest."

———

People of every kind continue to die in the southern deserts—adventure travelers, desert lovers, nature seekers—but the kind it kills most are still the Spanish speakers. It kills them more than ever, an average of nearly four hundred a year. Their deaths are so common that they make national news only when an especially large group gets lost and wiped out while on its way to a better opportunity. The names of the places they die are now also called sectors—Del Rio Sector, Marfa Sector, El Paso Sector—divisions of the U.S. Border Patrol, which usually finds the bodies. Their stories are case files.

Given the sheer volume of migrant fatalities, the U.S. Border Patrol seemed like the best place to begin a search for precedents of mercy killings in the desert. Almost every agent with a few years of field experience has come across the sad figure of a migrant's corpse curled up in the brush, a victim of dehydration or hypothermia. But while there are a few tales of lost migrants hanging themselves from trees, and plenty about bandits murdering isolated trekkers, there appear to be no documented cases of Kodikian-style mercy killings. Out of over a hundred active and retired agents who've served on the southern border, not one of them had ever encountered, or even heard of, a similar case.

"All of us have seen a lot," said Frank Hawkins, a retired Border Patrol agent with over twenty years in the field. "But it is very uncommon to see a mercy-killing or a suicide."

Hawkins, who is now a Episcopal priest in Rosenberg, Texas, believes the reasons for a lack of migrant mercy killings are very specific: "A smuggler puts together a group of aliens on the other side of the border. Among this herd are a few folks who may know each other or even be related to one another, but most groups are made up of total strangers. There may be a husband and wife traveling together, or two cousins, but they are only two out of a large group. The smuggler stresses the necessity of leaving behind anyone who can't physically endure the hardship of the trip."

"If an agent was to encounter [a mercy killing], I would think it would have made headlines," said another agent who's been on the border nine years. "I read about the Carlsbad situation, and I have a little trouble swallowing the story—that's my personal opinion."

Although there seem to be no documented cases of mercy killing in America's deserts, there's at least one story, unknown to anyone involved in the case, that is strikingly similar to Kodikian's. It comes from the Great Sahara, a desert so old, hot, and mercilessly vast that seventeen Chihuahuans could fit inside it. In 1991, the noted author William Langewiesche was visiting Tamanrasset, Algeria, when a local judge showed him a diary the police had recovered from the desert near the Niger border. It had belonged to a Belgian woman who perished along with her husband and five-year-old boy when their own road trip went terribly wrong. Although the diary itself is now lost in the turmoil that has since swept through that land, Langewiesche had a chance to read it, and wrote about the remarkable story it told in his book, *Sahara Unveiled*:

Partway to the border, as the desert descended into the great southern flats, the Belgians took a wrong turn. When they understood their mistake, they still had plenty of gas, and they set out to retrace their route. This was not easy, since the ground was hard-packed and rocky. But getting lost was part of the adventure, a memorable game for carefree Europeans. We know this because the woman later wrote it down. People dying of thirst in the desert often leave a written record. They have time to think. Writing denies the incredible isolation.

The Peugeot broke down. The Belgians rationed their water

and lay in the shade of a tarpaulin. The rationing did not extend their lives; they might as well have drunk their fill, since the human body loses water at a constant rate, even when dehydrated. The only way to stretch your life in the hot desert is to reduce your sweating: stay put, stay shaded, and keep your clothes on.

The Belgians hoped a truck would come along. For a week they waited, scanning the horizon for a dust-tail or the glint of a windshield. This was a place, more or less, where the maps still insist on showing a road. The woman felt the upwellings of panic. She began to write more frantically, filling pages in single sessions. The water ran low, then dry, and the family grew horribly thirsty. After filtering it through a cloth, they drank the car's radiator fluid. They arrived at the danger stage. . . .

After the radiator fluid was gone, the Belgians started sipping gasoline. You would too. Call it *petroposia*. Saharans have recommended it to me as a way to stay off battery acid. The woman wrote that it seemed to help. They also drank their urine. She reported that it was difficult at first, but that afterward it wasn't so bad.

The boy was the weakest, and was suffering terribly. In desperation, they burned their car, hoping someone would see the smoke. No one did. The boy could no longer swallow. His name was Maurice. His parents killed him to stop his pain. Later, the husband cut himself open and allowed his wife to drink his blood. At his request, she broke his neck with a rock. Alone now, she no longer wanted to live. Still, the Sahara was fabulous, she wrote, and she was glad to have come. She would do it again. She regretted only one thing—that she had not seen Sylvester Stallone in

Rambo III. Those were her last lines. She had lost her mind, but through her confusion must have remembered the ease of death in movies.

Movies, in fact, are the only places were mercy killing in survival situations seems common, specifically war movies. The scene in which a terminally wounded soldier begs a comrade in arms for a "mercy bullet" is frequent enough that we don't think twice when we see it, and Raffi would later say that his ordeal in Rattlesnake Canyon "was the closest thing to what I'd imagine combat is like." He probably got the analogy straight from Hollywood, because in real combat mercy killings are either not talked about or are extremely rare. Informal inquires on three different Vietnam veterans newsgroups visited by thousands produced not a single vet who had ever even heard of a mercy killing in combat, much less committed one. "That's Hollywood shit," one vet wrote about the mercy bullet scenario. "You keep on going till you can't go no more."

It would turn out that the closest thing to a legal precedent for Raffi's case came from maritime law. The sea, like the desert, can drive one to desperate acts, and over the centuries a few men have been prosecuted for committing homicides that, under the conditions, were morally defensible. One of the most infamous cases comes from Britain.

In 1884, a racing yacht named the *Mignonette* set sail from England, bound for Australia. The owner of the yacht had hired Captain Thomas Dudley and a crew of three other men to transport the ship all the way to Sydney, but they never made it. Far off the coast of West Africa, the *Mignonette* foundered in a storm and went to the bottom.

Dudley and his crew managed to escape in a dinghy, but their troubles were just beginning. They had almost no food and water, and, adrift hundreds of miles from the nearest shipping lane, their chances of survival were small. After nineteen days of seeing neither land nor sail, they were beyond desperate. They were starving and desiccated, their tongues black and swollen. The youngest member of the crew, a fourteen-year-old boy named Richard Parker, was particularly bad off, having drunk sea water despite the warnings of Dudley and the other men. As Parker lay semiconscious in the bow of the dinghy, Dudley made a decision that would go down in the history of criminal law.

Normally, castaways faced with death by starvation drew lots. The loser sacrificed his life for the others, who resorted to the taboo of cannibalism. The practice was common enough to have a term, "the custom of the sea," but Dudley and his crewmates forwent the formality of chance. Knowing that Parker was likely to die soon anyway, they cut his throat, drank his blood, and survived another eight days—long enough to be spotted and rescued by a German vessel, *The Horatio*.

Upon being rescued, Dudley told the *Horatio*'s captain—and later the British authorities—the truth. He could have hidden the killing easily, or even simply said that lots had been drawn, but he was a rigidly honest man. The British courts, which had long been searching for a case that would allow them to establish a harsh precedent against such practices, aggressively prosecuted Dudley and his first mate, Edwin Stephens, for murder. At their trial, *Regina v. Dudley and Stephens*, the crown rewarded Dudley's forthrightness by sentencing him and his first mate to death by hanging.

Luckily for the sailors, the public outcry against the sentence was so great that Queen Victoria immediately commuted the sentence to six months' hard labor. The men served their time, then lived out the rest of their lives haunted by the ghost of a fourteen-year-old boy.

16

In the weeks after the killing in Rattlesnake Canyon, Mark Maciha watched the incident evolve from a small newswire story out of Albuquerque into an international one. He now spent most of his time leading reporters and camera crews from as far as London down to the spot where Mattson had found Kodikian. Baby-sitting journalists, who often forgot to bring enough water themselves and had a way of turning the desert into an unnaturally noisy place, was not why he became a ranger. He preferred to be alone in the wilderness and cultivate its solitude. He put up with the reporters stoically, though, answering all their questions directly, with enough words to convey that he did not believe Raffi Kodikian's story.

"It just doesn't add up," was the quote he most often gave them. When they asked why, he let the landscape do his talking for him. He took them to the overlook where Mattson had first spotted the campsite, then pointed out that it had taken only ten minutes to walk to a point where the campsite could be seen. On the trail down, he stood them next to rock cairns and asked them to spot the next marker, which they always did. Once they reached the campsite, the reporters were confronted by a three-foot-high pile of stones, the same ones that had covered David Coughlin's body, and Maciha encouraged them to try lifting some of the bigger ones. After they hefted a few, groaning beneath their weight, he asked them whether they could imagine lifting *all* of those stones, then carrying them thirty feet if they'd had virtually no food or water for three days as Raffi had claimed. He would gesture to a six-hundred-foot peak behind him, and explain that if the friends had climbed it, they would have seen the road they came in on.

But he saved his best argument for last. He asked the reporters to lead the way out, and they usually managed to sniff out the trail while he followed behind. There was only one reporter, Bill Gifford from *Philadelphia Magazine*, whose tour resulted in an unfavorable impression of Maciha's theory. Gifford would later write that, during his visit, Maciha himself had led the way back, and walked right past the cairn marking the exit trail. "I always miss that," Gifford had quoted Maciha as saying.

A month after the killing, Maciha made his way down into the canyon again for the umpteenth time, this time carrying with him photographs that had been developed from David Coughlin's camera. In and of themselves they were unremarkable—shots of the canyon from various perspectives near the bottom. Two of them, however, showed the friends' tent, pitched and ready to be slept in, sitting in a completely different location than where the rangers had found them. Perhaps, Maciha wondered, if he could find the spot where the photographs were taken, he might find some remnant of their night there that would add another piece to the puzzle.

Once the ranger reached the canyon floor, he studied the photographs for points of reference—a familiar ridge line, promontory, or bend in the dry riverbed. Most of them seemed to be from a northern perspective, looking south, so he hiked north along the canyon floor, stopping every few minutes to line up another photograph. About a mile north of the access trail, he turned west up a side canyon, off the trail entirely. In the photos with the tent, there was a natural stone bench jutting out from a rock face, and after hiking another ten minutes he stopped dead in his tracks when he realized he was staring at exactly that.

There was no doubt about it: the friends had spent at least a night there. Maciha could even see a patch of cleared ground that still bore a slight impression from the tent. The ranger began searching the immediate vicinity, looking for anything they may have left behind. After about fifteen minutes of nosing around, he'd found a few boot prints, but other than the tent impression there was absolutely nothing. "Leave no trace . . ." the park's backcountry camping guidelines read. Except for the tent imprint, it appeared the friends had done exactly that.

Why had they come all the way up here? the ranger wondered as he prepared to head back. The spot was completely off the trail, isolated, a long way to go for a couple of guys who were supposedly planning on staying only one night. It would be another one of those prickly pear questions, the answer known only to Kodikian himself. By now Maciha was getting used to them.

As he turned to go, something on the ground caught the

ranger's eye. It was about twenty yards away, a paper of some kind, rammed into the spiny base of a sotol plant. He must have missed it on the way in as he was attempting to line up the rock formation with the photographs. When he got within a few feet of it, he knew what it was immediately. He had seen it a thousand times before. It was a Trails Illustrated topographical map of Carlsbad Caverns National Park, identical to the ones they sold back at the visitor center. The $7.95 price tag on the front of this one indicated that that was exactly where it had come from.

Maciha reached for it, careful to avoid the sotol spines protecting it as effectively as punji stakes. How it had gotten there was anybody's guess. Whether it was another work of the wind, or someone had intentionally hidden it, was impossible to tell. He placed it in a plastic bag.

———

After the reporters hiked down into Rattlesnake Canyon with Mark Maciha and fought to see the world through Kodikian's eyes, they usually swung back to Carlsbad and interviewed a man who never would, Chunky Click. He'd welcome them into his office, where they would immediately be confronted, everywhere they looked, by the face of John Wayne.

Click had been collecting Duke memorabilia since he was a kid, and when he became sheriff, he transferred as much of the collection as he could to his office. There were movie posters, autographed black-and-white still photos, line drawings, all of them framed. None of these, however, compared to the center-piece that sat immediately behind his desk: a bookshelf with seventeen china plates from the Franklin Mint, each with a different rendering of Wayne from one of his movies. There was Wayne bulldogging up the beach in *The Sands of Iwo Jima*, Wayne wielding one eye and a pistol in *True Grit*, Wayne the Searcher, Wayne the Flying Tiger. They gleamed like altarpieces. Click would talk Wayne as long as you liked.

Another thing that caught the eye were his pistols and gun belt. When he wasn't wearing them, they were usually hanging from the coat rack, two steely Colt .45s with butterscotch grips inlaid with Masonic emblems of silver, turquoise, and coral. His tooled leather gun belt, equally elaborate with his initials in silver and gold, had holsters specially crafted by inmates at the Terrell Unit, the prison in east Texas that hosts the state's death row. Click was friends with the warden. Getting the holsters properly sized had been tricky since Click couldn't just give the prisoners one of his guns. The sheriff solved the problem by laying a revolver on the Xerox machine and faxing a copy over to the prison. It was a no-nonsense solution, similar to the way he would come to view the Kodikian case.

"I don't care what anyone says," he professed, "people just don't do that to their friends. I wouldn't do that to my worst enemy. I believe he had every intention of killing him."

In the months immediately following the killing, the visceral disbelief Click had first felt upon reading the journal gradually became refined into a targeted argument as to why Kodikian's story, as he joked, "didn't hold water." Along with the arguments Mark Maciha was making about how Kodikian and Coughlin should have been able to find their way out of Rattlesnake Canyon, Click added crime scene evidence and what little he had learned about Kodikian's character. He had read Kodikian's '97 travel piece, and latched on to the episode where he nearly got lost in White Sands during the sandstorm.

"I think that's where he got the idea that he could have some kind of adventure in the desert, back in ninety-seven" the sheriff said. "He went to the desert on that trip, camped out in it. He knew what he was doing. He says so himself in that article that he spent only fourteen nights with a roof over his head. That means he camped out over fifty times. I don't care what anyone says, this guy was comfortable roughing it." (Conveniently enough, he left out the part where Kodikian returns to his car to find he'd locked his keys inside.)

One of the things that bothered Click most was the unopened can of beans the investigators had found. If the friends had been so desperate, Click said, then why hadn't they at least attempted to drink the syrupy water and sodium solution the beans were packed in? Severely dehydrated people had been known to drink a lot worse (the radiator coolant from Langewiesche's story comes to mind). "It would seem to me like the most basic thing," said the sheriff. "If you have water, or any kind of liquid, you'd try to drink it."

The sheriff was also quick to grab on to Maciha's discovery of what appeared to be their first night's campsite, a mile and half up the canyon. "That's an awful long way to go if you're just looking for a place to pitch a tent for the night," he said. "It's just one more thing." Could Kodikian have lured his friend off the trail, then intentionally hidden the map? Could they have been closet homosexuals in a lover's quarrel? The sheriff seemed certain the answer was anything but the one Raffi had already given.

Most troubling of all was the torched sleeping bag. Rattlesnake Canyon brimmed with brush fields and dry wood, including a dead walnut tree immediately behind the campsite where Mattson had found Kodikian. Why, Click wondered, had they bothered to burn something as tentatively flammable as a sleeping bag for a signal fire? Had they wanted to, they could have run around the canyon floor with a burning stick and started a wildfire so large that it would have been impossible not to notice. Faced with death, what man would hesitate at committing arson in the middle of nowhere?

Click saw only one explanation: "He killed him in his sleep, then burned the sleeping bag to hide the evidence."

Trace evidence from the crime lab in Albuquerque added weight to this argument; they had found sleeping bag fibers on the hilt of the folding knife Kodikian had used to kill Coughlin. Kodikian could have wiped the blade clean on the sleeping bag after he had used it for cutting cactus fruit, or their supposed suicide attempt, of course, but Gary McCandless—another Kodikian skeptic—doubted it. "The fact that the fibers were found on the hilt, and not in the stab wound or on the blade itself, makes sense," he said. "The fibers would have been pushed up into the hilt as the knife penetrated the bag, then Coughlin's chest."

Not even the journal, the strongest piece of evidence supporting Kodikian's story, made Click second-guess himself. He still pointed to what David Coughlin *hadn't* written in it as the most important insight it offered: "Never, not once, does Coughlin write in that notebook that he wanted to die, or that he wanted Raffi to kill him," he said.

"But what do I know?" he'd ask reporters after offering his speculations; "I'm just a redneck." The obvious analogy was that he had cast himself as the moral enforcer in an old western. There he was, sitting in his office surrounded by his Wayne posters, wearing his pistols and his star, playing the part everyone expected him to play: the straight-shootin' sheriff for whom everything was as black and white as a John Ford movie. Sometimes, when the answers eluded him, it seemed as if he would break character and admit that Kodikian *could* be telling the truth, but he'd remember himself. Somebody had to point out that, if Kodikian's story seemed unbelievable, the reason was probably because it just wasn't true.

All of these arguments sounded good—a crafty, cold-blooded murder was infinitely more accessible than the story Kodikian had told—but Gary Mitchell could atomize these theories unless the state provided the all-important motive. "There is a motive; we just haven't found it yet," Click was saying with a wink at the beginning of October, knowing full well that there was a police report citing Terry Connelly's statement about Coughlin and Swan having "been intimate." But by early November, neither Connelly nor Swan herself had come forward to confirm it, and with the trial less than two months away, Click was growing desperate.

As a last-ditch effort, he and McCandless decided to send Eddie Carrasco to Boston to team up with Travaglia for another round of questioning. It was a long shot, but maybe it was just what they needed to flush out the motive: a meeting between the city cop and the country cop.

———

Eddie Carrasco caught a flight east from El Paso on November 14. To save the county's money, he flew into Providence, Rhode Island, then rented a car and drove into Boston. It was the second time in his life he'd ever been to the East Coast. He got stuck in traffic for two hours on the way in, then lost in downtown Boston. In the end, he had to go to three different buildings, and ask directions from two different cops, before he found the FBI field office. Of course, some would say that happens to almost everybody who visits Boston.

Special Agent Travaglia was waiting for Carrasco, and the two men went right to work. Carrasco had only three days, so Travaglia had set up as many interviews as possible beforehand. Minutes after Carrasco arrived, Sonnet Frost walked into the office. She was friendly and open, and wanted to help, Carrasco could tell, but she had no more info than she had already told Travaglia. She found the "homosexual tension" theory totally improbable, a sentiment that would later be echoed by everyone who knew both men well. But she still had her doubts about Raffi's story. "As a result of the interview, Frost did express her skepticism to the defendant's account and suspected malicious intent or ulterior motives," he later wrote in his report. "However, Frost had no information or inferences by anyone to believe that was the case."

That afternoon, the two men drove out to Wellesley to interview the only man who had allegedly claimed to know of a possible ulterior motive: Terrance Connelly. The investigators had high hopes that together they could get the younger cop to affirm the statement he had supposedly made to Cunningham on August 9, about Coughlin and Swan "having been intimate on one occasion." If he was willing to swear to it and it was true, they might be able to confront Swan with his statement and see if she would admit to an affair.

Connelly has never consented to an interview, so accounts of the meetings come exclusively from Carrasco and Travaglia. According to them, as soon as the three of them sat down in the interview room at the Wellesley Police Department, the investigators' hopes began to vanish.

"During the interview, it became obvious Connolly's behavioral reactions were consistent as not being completely truthful," Carrasco stated in his report. "He [said he] never had any problem with the victim or the defendant or negative thoughts towards either. He heard only good about the defendant. No one ever told him or made an inference about the victim and Swan having a sexual relationship."

According to Carrasco, Travaglia became openly frustrated at Connelly. "He yelled at him," Carrasco recalled. "He said something to the effect of 'Hey, buster, that's not what you said when I talked to you before. This is serious business; a man is dead. You better start cooperating.' "

Carrasco asked him if he'd be willing to take a polygraph test. Connelly said he'd do it, but he wanted to talk to Chief Cunningham first. The interview fell apart, and the two investigators told him they'd come back the next morning.

After meeting with Connelly, Carrasco and Travaglia dropped by the Coughlin house on Pilgrim Road. The detective gave the Coughlins a large envelope containing Dave's clothes and personal items, and Bob Coughlin reiterated his belief in Kodikian's story, and told Carrasco that he thought the case might result in plea bargain.

"What are your feelings about that?" the detective asked.

"Well, before anything's done, I want to make sure that there's nothing else," Carrasco remembered Bob Coughlin saying.

When they returned to Wellesley the following day, Chief Cunningham joined the investigators and reminded Connelly, once again, about what he had said the day after the killing. And once again Connelly insisted that the chief had "misunderstood" him.

Eddie Carrasco asked Connelly again if he'd take a lie detector test; this time the young deputy hesitated. "He said something about wanting to talk to a lawyer first for advice," Carrasco recalled. The detective kept the heat on, asking him if he'd at least make a taped statement that could later be run through a computer voice stress analyzer. Terry Connelly demurred.

"I believe what happened was that Terry thought long and hard about the ramifications of his statement," Travaglia later said. "[He thought], 'Hey, I may be called as a witness in trial. I better really rethink my position.' "

Travaglia and Carrasco still had a thin hope that some of the people who had witnessed Connelly's earlier statement would confirm it and close a circle around him, but it soon became clear that the investigators were fighting a losing battle. Arnold Wakelin, the executive director for the town of Wellesley, "had no recollection" of Connelly even meeting with Cunningham. Chris Clark, the assistant director, did remember the meeting, but said that Connelly's answer to Cunningham's question about Coughlin and Swan having had a sexual relationship was more of an "impressionable shrug." Whether the Coughlins had been in contact with Connelly, or with David's coworkers at the town hall, is unknown, but it was clear that by November no one in Wellesley was vocalizing any doubt about Kodikian's story. A few months later, Connelly left his job at the Wellesley Police Department.

Both of the investigators were frustrated. "We were pretty well convinced that we did have a possible motive," said Travaglia. They had a practically unheard of reason for murder and, right beneath it, an alternative picture with dots that seemed just on the verge of connecting. They knew for certain that Dave Coughlin had spent a week in California with Raffi's ex-girlfriend. Maybe Raffi might have *told* Coughlin he didn't mind, but what guy, deep in his heart, wouldn't be just a bit bothered if his best friend took off with his ex for a week? And if Dave Coughlin had indeed told Terry Connelly that he'd actually *slept* with Swan, then maybe, facing death in Rattlesnake Canyon, he had told Raffi, too. It was just the kind of thing a man who thinks he's going to die might confess to a friend, and it wasn't hard to imagine all the heat, betrayal, and frustration Raffi was feeling exploding. Maybe Raffi had stabbed Dave in the heart because that was precisely where Coughlin had wounded him.

Carrasco's last hope was Swan herself. He had told her before leaving Carlsbad that he was coming to Boston and wanted to meet with her, and she had agreed, but after he arrived she left a message on Travaglia's answering machine saying that she had to leave town on a business trip. She left no forwarding number. On his last day in Boston, she called him at his hotel and said she couldn't meet with him until that evening. His plane was leaving in the afternoon. When he got back to Carlsbad, he tried to set up an interview with Swan over the phone, but there were more complications.

"I was never able to get her to commit to a time," he said.

The murder investigation was over.

17

It is said that Edward Marshall, a founding father of Bucks County, Pennsylvania, once walked sixty miles in a day and a half. He set out with two other men at sunrise on September 19, 1737, from the village of Wrightstown and headed northwest, up the Delaware Valley, at a relentless pace. By an agreement with the local Lanape Indians, the colonists were allowed to purchase as much land as a man could walk in thirty-six hours, and Marshall was one of three men who had been hand-picked to stake the claim. Five hundred acres of land was promised to the man who walked the farthest, but by noon the next day Marshall was the only one left. The two other walkers had fallen from exhaustion—one mortally. Marshall himself marched as promised till twelve P.M. and then collapsed; surveyors marked the spot and drew lines at right angles leading back to the Delaware River. The area the claim encompassed became known as the Walking Purchase, and it was bigger than the state of Rhode Island. The walk made Edward Marshall, at twenty-seven years old, a hero.

At twenty-five, Raffi Kodikian returned home to Bucks County more or less a villain. At worst, he was considered a cold-blooded murderer who had concocted an outlandish tale to hide his guilt; at best, he'd done something that to most people was just as unthinkable—ended his friend's life. The specifics of his ordeal, the unbearable loss of his friend and his own suffering in the canyon, mattered little to most people. He'd taken the Fifth, so few people knew his side of the story, and even if they had, it was questionable how much compassion he'd get from his community.

"I don't know all of the circumstances but if he were charged with murder, that is at least a malicious act and at worst it is an intentional, deliberate and premeditated act," Terry Houch, a Bucks County assistant district attorney, told the *Boston Herald* shortly after hearing that Kodikian was now at large in his district. Houch had followed the case in the local papers, and was stunned to learn that Judge Lyons had released Raffi on only $50,000 bail. "We have shaken-baby cases where the defense said it was an accident and we get at least six figures easily on bail," he went on to say. "Here, if he were charged with murder, he wouldn't get bail."

In Boston—Raffi's second home—headlines about the killing sparked rumors of a dark, violent past that led back to his college days. The most titillating of all conveniently connected him to one of the city's most famous unsolved and grisly crimes: the 1996 murder of Karina Holmer, a nineteen-year-old Swedish au pair whose severed torso was found in a Dumpster behind 1091 Boyleston Street, where Raffi was living at the time with Kirsten Swan. Raffi was never a suspect, and everyone in the building had been questioned at the time; but the *Boston Globe* now ran a story quoting local police as saying they were "taking another look" at Kodikian. The police later denied making the statement. The demonization of Kodikian appeared complete when the student newspaper he'd once written for, the *Northeastern News*, ran a story about the killing, along with an on-line poll: "If Raffi Kodikian is found guilty, should he get the death penalty?" it asked. Thirty-two percent of his responding alma mater answered yes.

Those who knew Raffi couldn't have been more opposed to the alternate theories, or surprised by news of the killing.

"I was in total shock," Craig Lewis remembered. "I found out about it the day before he was supposed to come back. I actually found out from some girls that are friends of mine that we had played pool with two weekends before. I thought they were pulling my leg, and that he was back at their apartment and they were like, 'Come on over, Craig, we gotta talk to you.' I just didn't believe them. And I was going over there, and I thought, 'You know, let me just go over to the supermarket and look at a newspaper.' It was right on the front page, I couldn't believe it. My buddy there in orange overalls with handcuffs."

"Bucks Man Charged in Slaying," "Slay Suspect Arrival Shocks Pennsylvania Officials," "Murder or Mercy?" were some of the headlines in the Philadelphia and Boston papers greeting him upon his return. Raffi had expected to write the news—not make it—and now, on top of his grief, he found himself having to avoid the very group of people he once considered colleagues. Hardly a day went by when a reporter or a television crew didn't come knocking. He kept well out of sight while his mother, sister, or father answered the door and politely refused to comment. Once, on a sweltering Indian summer day when a local TV crew, along with some newspaper reporters, were camped out in front of the house, his mom even brought them lemonade, but declined to answer their questions.

The media seemed to be everywhere. A few weeks after he got back, Raffi drove up to Boston to collect some of his belongings. When he and Craig Lewis drove by his apartment in West Roxbury, they saw reporters camped out in front, and ended up having to sneak around through the back. Raffi had shrugged it off as a joke, but Lewis knew the pressure was taking its toll.

"When stuff's eating him up inside, he keeps it to himself," Lewis said; he remembered a day a year earlier when he and Raffi had been working out in the gym, and his friend had been unusually silent and remote. It was only when he pressed him about it that Raffi told him his uncle had died. Lewis said that a similar silence overtook Raffi later that day, after they had picked up his things and were driving around town. Lewis knew what the problem was this time.

"I miss Dave," Raffi finally said.

Raffi tried to stay busy while he waited for the trial. There was only one place he could work: Rental World. He'd worked at his father's business before, during high school; it had been just a temporary job then, but now he was looking at the prospect of working in the family business for the rest of his life. Hal thought it would be a good idea to get him out in the world again, so in February, three months before his trial was scheduled to begin, he sent his son to the annual American Rental Association convention in Anaheim, California.

Raffi went with two other employees, including Sharon Osinski, a woman who had worked for Hal for eleven years and had known Raffi since he was a kid. They stayed in a hotel across the street from the convention center, a massive glass hall next to Disneyland. Every morning they would cross the street to the center, and one morning as they crossed they heard a tremendous noise.

"We all turned around and this car had flipped over on its hood," Osinski remembered. "The first thing Raffi did was just throw his stuff down and run toward the car."

Raffi was the first one to reach the vehicle. Inside he found its driver, a woman, pinned upside down and bleeding.

"It took twenty minutes for the ambulance to come," Osinski said. "He held her hand and comforted her the whole time. She was crying the whole time and Raffi was saying, 'It's okay, it's okay, there's just a little blood.' I was really taken by the whole thing. And I'm looking at him knowing what he just went through and I'm like, 'There's not a mean bone in this man's body.' "

Sharon Osinski thought to herself that if she were in trouble someplace, she'd want Raffi with her. She would trust him.

18

The sputtering, inconclusive end of the murder investigation supported Raffi's claim that Coughlin's death was indeed a mercy killing, but Gary Mitchell knew all too well that, under the law, his client was still far from finding mercy himself. Les Williams had said it: "You do not get to kill someone in New Mexico just because they ask you to." It was ironic, because every other headline about the killing read "Murder or Mercy?," but as far as state and federal law was concerned, there wasn't a difference.

The closest any state came to allowing mercy killing was Oregon, which had passed a referendum a year earlier legalizing physician-assisted suicide. But a licensed doctor administering lethal drugs to a terminally ill patient was quite different from a would-be travel writer winging it in the desert with a buck knife. Raffi would have been charged with murder even in Oregon, and he could have been charged with murder in other states even if he'd been a physician and David was terminally ill. Less than two weeks after Raffi killed David, in fact, a New Mexico grand jury did just that when it charged Georges Reding, a doctor and good friend of Jack Kevorkian, with the 1998 death of Donna Brennan, a multiple sclerosis sufferer from Rio Rancho.

Mitchell had followed the Rio Rancho case, and the Kevorkian cases before that, with great interest. Even while he saved the men on death row from lethal injection, he staunchly believed that the rest of us, if suffering and terminally ill, had a right to ask for the same thing. He sat on the board of directors at his local hospital, and was part of a group of lawyers actively lobbying legislators in Albuquerque to get physician-assisted suicide legalized in the state. Kevorkian had finally been convicted of murder in Michigan only that March, but Mitchell was more interested in the fact that three other juries had refused to convict him of assisted suicide, despite overwhelming evidence. Mercy killing may be murder according to the law, but in people's minds—and juries were made of people—there were more than two thousand years of philosophical, ethical, and legal arguments suggesting the two acts were perceived quite differently.

"Mercy killing" is roughly defined as "the compassionate taking of another life in order to end its suffering." It's the broadest term of a moral construct that includes all acts of "euthanasia," an ancient Greek word meaning "good death." We now mainly associate euthanasia with the bringing about of a gentle and easy death in the case of an incurable and painful disease, and modern ethics holds that in order for euthanasia to be morally defensible, it must first meet some basic requirements. The request for death has to come from a person who is in full possession of his faculties, and death otherwise must be slow, painful, and inevitable. There can be no question of surviving.

Under those conditions, Raffi's case fit the ethical requirements marginally at best: Dave didn't have a disease, it was unknown how lucid he actually was at the time he begged for death, and in hindsight his death was far from inevitable. But Raffi and David didn't have the luxury of hindsight in Rattlesnake Canyon, and therein was the argument Mitchell could make: in a way, David's severe dehydration was *like* a disease; he was suffering, and after three lost days it was reasonable for the friends to believe that death was indeed inevitable. David L. Perry, director of ethics programs at Markkula Center for Applied Ethics at Santa Clara University, explained: "If David Coughlin reasonably believed that he was going to die in the desert, and saw his remaining hours as containing nothing but increasing misery and degradation, then shortening his life would not necessarily deprive him of anything he valued or could value. And if he were too weak to take his own life, he could waive his right not to be killed and ask his friend to do it, without thereby placing an intolerable ethical burden on his friend. In that case, we might still technically label Raffi's action as a homicide (the intentional killing of a human being), but morally we should not consider it murder or an unjust killing."

From the beginning, Mitchell saw Raffi's as a euthanasia case. "I don't view this case as a criminal matter," he said in October. "I view this case as one of those where people have had a loved one who was dying. We had two or three cases where we got a court order to remove life support. I view this case very similar."

Mitchell's impassioned interviews sat well with the media;

there was no doubt about the sincerity and compassion he had for his client. In the court of public opinion, at least, he was able to get a few people to think differently about Raffi, to force them to imagine themselves in his shoes. But there was only one problem.

He could woo a jury until their hearts bled with compassion for Raffi's ordeal in the canyon, but at the end of day the judge was obligated to instruct them to disregard his entire argument. "Mercy" was not an admissible defense; if they believed it was a mercy killing, then the letter of the law commanded them to convict for murder. His best hope with a mercy argument was the legal equivalent of the long bomb: a jury nullification, in which the jury simply ignored the judge and the law and ruled according to their conscience, but by law he was forbidden to tell them that the option even existed. They'd have to reach that conclusion on their own, and the judge could always declare a mistrial. The next best outcome was a hung jury, but good defense attorneys don't bet on juries hanging or nullifying, especially when their clients are from out of town; they bet on not-guilty verdicts with arguments based solidly on the evidence and the law.

Mitchell bought as much time as he could for Raffi. The basic law in New Mexico is that a case has to go to trial within six months, but he was able to wrangle and get it pushed back from January 3, 2000, to April 30. But all the time in the world wasn't going to change the fact that a euthanasia defense, no matter how good, just wasn't going to fly with a judge. In early February, as Mitchell began preparing in earnest, he finally had to accept that he'd have to replace the euthanasia story he'd been telling the press with a defense that the judge would actually allow. After seven months of selling mercy, he was totally blank as to what that

would be. So he walked down the hall to the office of Shawn
Boyne, a whip-smart lawyer whom he'd hired eight months earlier.

"Raffi's in serious trouble because we don't have any mercy-
killing statute," he told her with a grave, panicked look on his
face. "You're going to have to invent something."

———————

Shawn Boyne had seen that look before. Her boss had been pressed
for time ever since she'd started working for him the previous
spring, after she responded to a Help Wanted ad he'd placed in several New Mexico papers.

"It was a very bizarre ad," Boyne remembered, "It said something like, 'Do you want to fight for the downtrodden?' It was an
advertisement for a 'Don Quixote type' lawyer."

The Quixote reference struck a chord. At forty-two years old,
Boyne's career had been as much of a crusade as Mitchell's. Originally
from Wisconsin, she had gotten a law degree from USC, then taken a
job in a public defender's office in Watts, Los Angeles, right when the
crack wars were wreaking their havoc on the community. Like a lot of
young lawyers, racking up case experience was as much a motivation
for taking the job as idealism, but the experience taught her something she would never forget: those who don't have the money to pay
for a good lawyer invariably get longer prison sentences. And, like a
lot of public defenders, she eventually burned out.

She had seen New Mexico for the first time while on a road
trip almost identical to the one Kodikian and Coughlin had been
making—from Boston to L.A.—and fallen in love with its explo-
sive landscape. It had never left her mind all throughout law
school and her time in Watts, so when she quit the public

defender's office she drove back and took the first job she could find, at a district attorney's office in Farmington. Once she had some prosecuting experience under her belt, Boyne moved on to another district attorney's office, this time in Taos, where she had always wanted to live. Her work there, prosecuting domestic violence and child-abuse cases, satisfied her in terms of activism, but Shawn Boyne had an admitted nose for trouble. In Taos, Boyne claimed, she noticed that some of the cases moving through the district attorney's office weren't being prosecuted, and she called the FBI when she realized that the defendants were friends and relatives of prosecutors and local politicians. She said the Taos district attorney fired her as a result of her queries, and the FBI had nothing to go on because the critical files mysteriously disappeared in a robbery of the office. But Boyne was just getting started. She rolled up her sleeves, filed a wrongful-termination case, and began campaigning for her former boss's opponent in the upcoming election. The case was settled, and her old boss lost his reelection bid.

"I ended up being forced into private practice because no D.A. in the state would hire me," she said. "I also ran for judge up in Taos, but didn't win, and decided I wanted to get the hell out of Dodge."

It was right about then that she saw Gary Mitchell's Don Quixote ad.

"I hadn't thought much of becoming a criminal defense lawyer," she said, "but I had no choice."

She sent Mitchell her resume. He called her a few weeks later on a Sunday night at around ten-thirty. He had read about her in newspaper stories about the Taos scandals, and had also heard of her through one of his best friends, Joe Shattuck.

"He said, 'This is Gary Mitchell,' and I didn't believe him,"

Boyne recalled. "I told him that Gary Mitchell wouldn't call me at ten-thirty on a Sunday night. Then I said to him, 'You're at the office. This sounds like a job I'm not interested in.' I don't think he was used to anybody giving him shit like that. But it really was Gary Mitchell."

A few days later, she drove down to Ruidoso, and he gave her the job.

Boyne had worked no more than three murder cases since then, and on those she had mostly assisted. Asking her to come up with a defense in any murder trial would have been placing a lot on her shoulders, but asking her to find one for Kodikian was like asking her to identify what species a bird with fins belonged to, then convince a judge and jury the creature wasn't from another planet. She needed a defense that in some elastic way fit the facts of Kodikian's case. She had no idea what to do, so she started at square one by whipping out a copy of New Mexico's jury instruction booklet and writing out a list of all the complete defenses for murder.

It didn't take her long: there were only six complete defenses for murder in New Mexico:

Alibi
Entrapment
Self-defense
Duress
Insanity
Involuntary Intoxication

Because Kodikian had already admitted to a mercy killing, most of the defenses on the list—alibi, entrapment, self-defense, duress—were immediately out. Insanity was getting warmer—they could argue that the desert heat had driven him mad—but it usually required a long-term condition, and Raffi didn't have a diagnosed history of becoming homicidal every time he got thirsty. (Temporary insanity, another good option, wasn't even on the list. The state of New Mexico does not consider it a complete defense; all it does is lower the charge to second-degree murder).

Her eyes settled on involuntary intoxication.

She'd barely even heard of it. It was a fairly new defense that had cropped up in the wake of the explosion of both illicit and prescription drugs in the last thirty years. There'd been some rare cases in which defendants had been secretly dosed with drugs, or even been prescribed a drug, that had caused them to become murderously violent or negligent in their actions. Since they'd had no idea they were under the influence in the first place, they obviously couldn't be held accountable for their actions.

She pulled out Raffi's medical records from the file that Mitchell had handed her. At first glance, Raffi seemed like a poor candidate for an involuntary intoxication defense—he hadn't been prescribed anything, and his blood work had shown negative for drugs. But there were substances he had in overabundance, namely sodium, which had risen in concentration as his water level dropped. His sodium level of 174, in fact, was 22 to 16 percent higher than normal, more than enough to cause sodium poisoning. Boyne quickly got on the World Wide Web and looked up the symptoms of sodium poisoning. Severe mental impairment was a primary result.

In the brain, sodium acts as an electrolyte, working in conjunction with potassium to conduct signals between neurons. When it becomes too concentrated, not only can the signals become disrupted, but cells in the brain (and elsewhere in the body) can become damaged as they dump their water into the blood to maintain osmotic equilibrium. The condition is called hypernatremia, a fancy word for dehydration of the brain. It is precisely the same condition that causes sailors lost at sea to go mad after they've ingested salt water. Raffi hadn't drunk seawater, but his resultant state was the same. He'd become intoxicated—against his will or knowledge—by his own salt.

An hour later, she walked into Mitchell's office.

"I found a defense. It's involuntary intoxication."

Mitchell just stared at her as she explained, his face as wooden as the knots in his desk. For a moment Boyne thought she would have to start looking in the Help Wanted sections again.

"Brilliant," he finally said.

————

However clever the defense was, it was still a long shot, because the involuntary intoxication defense itself was almost unheard of. Involuntary intoxication had not only never been used in a dehydration case in New Mexico, it had never been used in the state, period, and had been used only a relative handful of times in the history of American law. In New Mexico's jury instruction book, Boyne even saw a footnote that said, "Some commentators have suggested that the defense is non-existent." Using it in a case where no drugs had been taken had never been done. The legal definition of intoxication was also a problem. *Black's Law Dictionary* defined it as "a disturbance of mental or physical capacities resulting from the *introduction* of substances into the body." Since Raffi hadn't actually ingested anything, there was no way they could use the defense in a courtroom without first getting Judge Forbes to approve it in a pretrial motion.

With less than two months to go until trial, Boyne began putting the motion together by interviewing as many experts and case law references as possible. She had no problem finding doctors who could confirm that, based on his sodium level, there was a high probability that Raffi had hypernatremia. She also discovered that their best possible shot at getting the judge to disregard the "ingestion" problem was, oddly enough, *hypo*natremia, or the exact opposite of having too much sodium. Its symptoms were virtually identical—it was merely an imbalance in the opposite direction. Most important, there were drugs that could cause it, namely diuretics. Theoretically, Raffi could have ingested a diuretic and wound up with the same mental impairment. If the resultant state was the same, she would argue, then ingestion was incidental.

While Boyne and Mitchell prepared their motion, they also realized that it didn't make much sense for the state of New Mexico to recognize involuntary intoxication as a complete defense, but not temporary insanity. As they aptly put in their motion: "Essentially, involuntary intoxication occurs when an individual becomes temporarily insane without his knowledge or consent." Since they were already throwing a bomb, they decided to go for broke and ask Judge Forbes to be the first judge in the state ever to allow temporary insanity as a complete defense. If he felt uncomfortable presiding over the state's first involuntary intoxication case, maybe he'd feel better calling it something else. They submitted their memorandum in a hearing at the district court on March 28, 2000. Raffi's fate now depended on whether or not Judge Forbes would allow both or either defense. If he did,

Mitchell and Boyne were almost certain they could convince a jury to let Kodikian walk. But without a ruling accepting temporary insanity as a complete defense, or jury instruction allowing their use of involuntary intoxication, odds were Raffi was at best looking at conviction for second-degree murder, which could cost him fifteen years in prison—and at worst, life. Judge Forbes told them to come back for his answer in three weeks.

The wind was roaring outside the king cab as they made the 150-mile drive back to Ruidoso. They had just passed Artesia, which lies about midway between Carlsbad and Roswell on US 285, when Mitchell suddenly screeched to a halt and turned the truck around.

"What's going on?" Boyne asked.

"We just passed one of our witnesses," he said.

But Boyne saw no one, not even a car. Then Mitchell pointed to a sign on the other side of the road. It was a historical marker for one of the many Spanish expeditions that had passed through hundreds of years ago.

"I'm gonna call the University of New Mexico history department and see if anybody in that conquistador's army died of dehydration," he said. Boyne rolled her eyes.

She knew her boss would revel in wowing a jury with yarns about dead Spaniards, but when they came back to earth, they'd acquit Raffi based on the unvarnished principles of organic chemistry.

———

Two days later, as Raffi waited for news back in Pennsylvania, Mitchell and Boyne drove back to Carlsbad to hear Judge Forbes's response to their motion.

"The Court acknowledges that this case presents unique factual circumstances that have never been seen before in the State of New Mexico or in other jurisdictions," he began. "The Defendant first asks this Court to allow the use of temporary insanity as a complete defense. New Mexico does not recognize the use of temporary insanity as a defense, for the insanity defense in New Mexico requires that the insanity be of a prolonged nature. . . ."

It had taken him only twenty seconds to knock down their first request. So far, he was sticking to the letter of the law. They were not yet discouraged, however, because they both knew that the temporary insanity request was a wild pitch anyway. Half the reason they had put it in the motion in the first place was to give him something to shoot down so that by the time he got to their second request—involuntary intoxication—he might be a bit more open-minded. Boyne held her breath.

"The Defendant appears to concede that New Mexico does not allow for a temporary insanity instruction," he continued, "and therefore asks this Court to adopt an instruction on involuntary intoxication based on the Defendant's level of dehydration. The Court does not dispute the Defendant's extensive research on involuntary intoxication, but the essential question is whether the facts of this particular case allow for an involuntary intoxication instruction, regardless of whether it is a complete defense or not. In order to answer the fundamental question in this Motion, the Court needs to decipher exactly what is meant by the term 'intoxication.' "

Mitchell's and Boyne's hearts sank as Judge Forbes quoted the definition of intoxication from *Black's Law Dictionary*, then the one from the state's penal code, then another from a state supreme court case. Ingestion. Ingestion. Ingestion.

"All of these definitions of intoxication call for a substance being ingested or introduced into the body. It is clear that there was no intoxication in this case. A quote from the Defendant's Motion on page sixteen is useful in the Court's analysis. 'The leap from using ingesting of a substance to form the basis of involuntary intoxication to dehydration is a small one.' The Court agrees that the Defendant's argument is a 'leap' and is a leap, no matter how big or small, that this Court is not prepared to recognize."

————

Les Williams was satisfied with judge's ruling; it had been almost identical to his own response to Mitchell and Boyne's motion. But he took no delight in the prospect of putting away a man for life for a crime whose intent he couldn't be sure was evil. Back in November, after the murder investigation turned up nothing, he and Mitchell had talked about the possibility of things coming down a plea bargain. Now they quickly formalized one.

Mitchell explained the details to Raffi later that afternoon: If Raffi pled guilty to second-degree murder, Williams would allow him to retain his right to appeal Judge Forbes's ruling on the involuntary intoxication motion. If Raffi took the deal, they'd go straight to a sentencing hearing, but it would by no means be a typical one. Judge Forbes was well aware of the unusual nature of this case, and he was prepared to hear extensive testimony and argument, far more than was typical during a sentencing hearing. The involuntary intoxication and temporary insanity defenses might not be admissible in a trial, but he and Boyne could certainly use them in a sentencing hearing. In effect, it would be very similar to a trial. Instead of persuading a jury to issue a not-guilty verdict, they would try to persuade Judge Forbes to suspend or defer his sentence.

Raffi didn't like the idea. In his mind, he had no choice but to give Dave the death he wanted in Rattlesnake Canyon, and conceding that it was criminal smacked of betrayal, to Dave, to himself, and to the truth of his intentions. Mitchell told him that he probably wouldn't get the full fifteen years, but anything was possible. Judge Forbes had so far been unbending. And if he took the plea bargain, he would end up explaining the felony conviction for the rest of his life. How many people would understand? The journalist in Raffi knew that, however organic it had been for him, from the outside his story was outlandish. But there it was: if he didn't take the plea, he would have to explain it to a jury anyway; if they didn't believe him, he might get life in prison. Even if they did believe him, they could easily convict him on the principle of the law. A long incarceration would destroy his family. They would hurt even more than they hurt now.

He took the deal.

19

Anyone watching the evening news in early May 2000 saw the live aerial footage: an immense ponderosa forest curtained in smoke, and rapidly disintegrating as one-hundred-foot-high trees ignited and vanished as fast as kindling in a campfire. By the middle of the week of May 8, the Cerro Grande blaze was ominously closing in on the town of Los Alamos, and the nation watched in excitement and dread as first one house, then whole blocks and neighborhoods were overrun by the blaze. Raffi Kodikian's sentencing hearing, which took place the same week three hundred miles away in Carlsbad, didn't stand a chance against that kind of drama. So it was that few outside of New Mexico ever heard his long-awaited testimony, or learned of the punishment handed out to him.

Raffi entered the courtroom shortly before nine. He looked nothing like the worn-out suspect from the mug shot. He had the obligatory courtroom haircut, close on the sides, slightly longer and stylishly choppy on top. He was wearing a black suit and a blue shirt, what could have passed as wedding attire. Every eye in the audience was on him, scanning his face for signs of a hidden truth. Some say you can tell a man's guilt by his eyes, but Kodikian's must have been more like mirrors than windows: everybody saw something different. Murderous rage, ingenious deception, absolute compassion—his black irises gave back nothing, and in that nothing, individual opinions found their confirmation.

The courtroom had two columns of wooden church-style benches for the public that ran about ten rows deep. Hanging from thick crossbeams were six antique wrought-iron and stained-glass chandeliers, touches of the Old West that kept the audience in relative dimness compared to the courtroom's well, which was awash in modern fluorescent lighting.

Since Kodikian had accepted the plea bargain, the jury box sat empty, but the audience was full of journalists. Reporters from the *Denver Post*, the AP, the *Albuquerque Journal*, and the Boston papers—the *Globe* and the *Herald*—were all there, along with Kyle Marksteiner, the reporter who had been covering the story for the *Carlsbad Current-Argus* since the day after Kodikian was arrested. It was the biggest herd of newspeople the town had ever seen. Judge Forbes had allowed a pool video camera to be present in the courtroom, and outside two white satellite trucks gleamed on the edge of the courthouse lawn, announcing the hoopla to the cars passing by on Canal Street. *Dateline*, *20/20*, and *Inside Edition* were all on hand—each planned to air features on the case, and unbeknownst to any of the other reporters, one of them already had a scoop.

A week earlier, Raffi had given the only interview he'd give about the case to *20/20*'s Connie Chung, who flew out to New Mexico and met with Kodikian and his family in Mitchell's office.

"It was his idea, he wanted to do it," Mitchell said of Raffi's decision to talk. In what would be one of the most intense interviews Chung ever conducted, Raffi brought a cameraman, and two of Mitchell's secretaries, to tears. Chung herself was also deeply moved but reserved judgment.

"There were people who came to conclusions," Chung said, "but I couldn't. For thirty years I've trained myself to try and be objective. If I do have a bias, I bend over backwards the other way. If I have a thought or opinion, I bend the other way. I believed the sheriff when I heard his argument, then I believed Raffi when I heard him. . . . But I'm awful," she said with an apologetic laugh. "I always believe the last person I talked to."

Chung was off on another story by the time the hearing started, but the rest of the reporters filled the front rows on the right side of the gallery, clutching their notepads and speculating as to the identities of the people across the aisle, behind Kodikian. A dozen friends and family members had come to support him, and there was a general understanding that no one else was welcome over there. Over time, their collective vow not to speak to the media had hardened into something close to disdain, despite—or perhaps because of—the obvious irony of Kodikian himself being a journalist. Judge Forbes called the court to order, and asked Kodikian to approach the podium.

The judge was a methodical and careful man who fully believed that there was no better alternative to justice than a rigorous trial by jury. He knew that Kodikian's punishment was one of the most difficult legal decisions in the history of the state and had no desire to make it on his own. As he explained the rights Kodikian was surrendering by pleading no contest to second-degree murder, he emphasized the gravity of leaving his fate up to a single judge. When he was finished, he looked long and hard at Kodikian, almost as if expecting him to change his mind.

"Now that I have gone through those constitutional rights that you're waiving . . . do you *still* want to continue in this no-contest plea?" he asked.

"My lawyer, Mr. Mitchell, has advised me that this would be the best path to take," Kodikian said, hesitating to acknowledge his own complicity in the plea. Then, after the slightest pause, he quickly blurted out, "Yes, sir."

———

Lance Mattson, the ranger who had found Kodikian on the afternoon of August 8, was the prosecution's first witness. He took the stand in his ranger's uniform and described how he had learned of the missing hikers, gone down into the canyon, and encountered Kodikian lying alone in the tent. He recalled Kodikian asking him for water and pointing to the pile of rocks where Coughlin's body was buried, then described turning up the stone that revealed Coughlin's shirt-covered face. As he told of treating Kodikian, and the conversation they had while in the canyon, Deputy District Attorney Les Williams narrowed in on what would be his main contention throughout the hearing—that Kodikian had been fully aware of his own actions.

"So what would you say his mental state was from the time that you found him to the point that we're talking about right now?" Williams asked.

"Through my examinations and with my level of training I did feel he was dehydrated," Mattson replied. "The only evidence to

Dave (left), Kirsten, and Raffi.

The friends strike a pose
for a photo in downtown
Philadelphia on New
Year's Day, 1999.

A view of the dry riverbed from the lower slopes of Rattlesnake Canyon, not far from the old ranch foundation. The far ridge marks the canyon's southern terminus, a mere half mile away.

(JASON KERSTEN)

A lonely mesquite atop Rattlesnake Canyon's western plateau provides some of the only shade around. This could very well be the same tree the friends lay beneath after climbing out of the canyon on Friday, August 6. Visible in the distance are the desert plains.

(JASON KERSTEN)

The remains of the SOS signal the friends built on Saturday, August 7.
(JIM'S PHOTOGRAPHY)

Minutes after being discovered, Kodikian lies back in the tent while Park Ranger Lance Mattson provides medical aid.

Raffi Kodikian is escorted to Eddy County Magistrate's Court by Sheriff M. A. "Chunky" Click (left), Chief Detective Gary MacCandless (right), and Deputy Ron Tackett (far right).

RIGHT: *Mark Anthony "Chunky" Click, the sheriff of Eddy County.*
(PHILIP JONES GRIFFITHS)

BELOW: *Defense Attorney Gary Mitchell.*
(PHILIP JONES GRIFFITHS)

ABOVE: *Carlsbad Deputy District Attorney Lesley Williams.*
(PHILIP JONES GRIFFITHS)

BELOW: *Park Ranger Mark Maciha, next to a cairn marking the spot where David Coughlin's body was found. The rocks, some of which easily weigh fifty pounds, came from both Coughlin's grave and the SOS signal. "If they had the strength to lift these rocks, why couldn't they walk out?" Maciha would find himself asking.*
(PHILIP JONES GRIFFITHS)

Raffi shields his eyes while video of Coughlin's cowboy grave is played in court. (AP)

The murder weapon, alongside a page in the journal.

(JIM'S PHOTOGRAPHY)

give me any idea of mental state was whenever I asked a question Mr. Kodikian was slow in responding, like he was thinking about it. But every question I asked he produced an answer. 'Where is your identification?' He thought about it and produced it. He knew what I was saying and I knew exactly what he was saying."

Williams finished with him a few minutes later, ending his examination by having Mattson recall Kodikian's statements about how he and Coughlin had attempted to kill themselves, failing because their "knives were too dull." After the prosecutor relinquished the podium, there was a sense among the reporters that the ranger's testimony—filled with qualifiers and far more guarded than anyone had expected—had done more for the defense than for the prosecution.

Gary Mitchell took his time cross-examining the ranger. Addressing him by his first name, he used Mattson as an expert on the general features of the park, deferring to his backcountry knowledge. His informal, supportive tone seemed to bring the ranger into a more conversational mode, and soon Mitchell was homing in on the park's policies.

"Now, as part of the preparation, or the availability of water at the National Park Service at Carlsbad, do they sell water there?" he asked the ranger.

"The concession there, the restaurant there, does sell water in small containers."

"A dollar thirty-eight for a pint of water?"

"I believe so. I'm not sure of the price."

"So if I'm going overnight, my buddy and I are going overnight, that's about twenty-seven dollars worth of water we've got to buy at [the visitor center]?"

"If that's what the numbers add up to . . . I'm not sure," said Mattson.

"I think that's about what they add up to. That's a pretty good concession!" Mitchell said wryly.

Mitchell next focused on the fifteen-inch-high rock cairns that mark Rattlesnake Canyon's trails. He carefully led Mattson into reluctantly admitting that, "to some people," the cairns can be difficult to spot, especially the ones marking the exit trail, because they meet the canyon floor in a place that is already covered by thousands of identical stones. Once Mitchell had established the conceivability of the friends getting lost, he then brought Mattson to the question of dehydration. The ranger admitted that when he found Kodikian, he concluded that he had "the classic signs of dehydration." His skin had tented, his pulse was elevated, and he had vomited three times while the ranger attempted to give him water.

Mitchell's final line of questioning was perhaps the most damaging. It centered on the camping permit the friends had filled out.

"Was there some method in which you checked up on these permits to see if people had returned?" he asked.

"No. It's just the observations of the rangers working at the park."

"I see. So if I fill out a permit there and hand it in, the rangers don't observe that I've returned. There's not some system by which that permit is turned in, saying, 'Listen, we've got campers there a day overdue' or 'They're two days overdue.' There's not some system at Carlsbad for that?"

"At that time, no sir, there isn't."

"Okay. So if you're camping out there and you're wondering if somebody's coming, the fact of the matter is that, unless some of the rangers spot it, they may not be coming."

"That is possible, yes sir."

Mitchell walked back to the defense table with a loose stride. Williams now needed to fight hard to get his witness back. He began his redirect by picking up where he had left off, asking the ranger to describe the cuts he had seen on Kodikian's wrists.

"It looked to me about an eighth of an inch," Mattson said. "It was . . . it looked like it had penetrated the skin, but it was not bleeding. It was just kind of at that boundary between that point."

"So no blood? You didn't see any blood on his wrists?"

"No, not that I remember."

It wasn't until after he got Mattson to restate that he thought Kodikian was "alert" that he finally brought his witness back to the cairns.

"And these markers on the trail, the cairns, the little rock piles . . . The way the defense talked . . . I mean, can you tell that they're artificial piles of rock?"

"To me, sir, yes. I can tell. They're piled up."

"Now the defense talked about buying the water bottles. Is there water available to visitors to the park that they don't have to purchase? Water fountains, water faucets, things of that kind?"

"There are water faucets and fountains in the bathroom, yes sir."

"So you don't have to buy water?"

"No."

"I have no further questions."

———

Second on the stand was John Keebler, the sixty-nine-year-old park volunteer who had spotted Coughlin's car at the trailhead on August 8. He'd never been interviewed by the media, and hadn't even been mentioned by name in any of the news stories about the case. The general feeling among the reporters was that he'd been a small-time player, a mild-mannered man who loved the park, happened to notice a car, and unwittingly stumbled into a scene that nobody—not to mention a volunteer in his golden years—should have had to witness.

"So what did you do after you saw the car there?" Williams asked.

"Well, I'd heard over the park radio Wednesday that the permit had been issued," he said in a slow and graveled voice, "and with that I knew that they were still out there. So I went over to the visitor center and had lunch, then I went and found Lance Mattson and told him about it, that I thought they were well overdue."

Keebler described the ensuing trek down into the canyon and the discovery of Kodikian, whom he referred to as "Raffi." At one point, Mattson had left him alone with Raffi while he climbed a nearby slope to get better radio reception.

"When you were with him, did you talk to him?" Williams asked.

"Yes, some. He was talkative. That's when he was drinking his water and he said, 'How much should I drink?' And I said, 'Well, take it easy.' At that time he'd already drunk about a quarter of a canteen and then again vomited. And that's when, after Lance had already found the gravesite, that he told me he killed his best friend this morning."

"Did you ask him about that, or did he just volunteer it?"

"He volunteered it. He just told me."

"Did he tell you how he did that?"

"No. I'd overheard him before tell Lance, 'That knife over there,' the one that was by the side of the tent."

Williams walked over to the evidence table and picked something up.

"You said, 'that knife.' Were you referring to this knife, marked state's exhibit one?"

"That looks like it, yes."

"Did he tell you anything else?"

"Well, there in the conversation he told me that he had tried to take his own life, and he showed me his wrist, where he had some marks on his wrist. And he said, 'My knife was too dull; I couldn't take my life.' "

"And when you were speaking with him, did he seem like he knew what you were saying?"

"Yes, he did."

"And did you understand him?"

"Very clearly."

"I have no further questions."

Shawn Boyne, who had been quietly taking notes by Mitchell's side, now rose and quickly took the podium, arching her shoulders toward the stand. She had the lip-licking interest of a cheetah who had just spotted a wildebeest staggering behind the pack.

"Sir, I am understanding your testimony correctly that on August fourth, that very evening, that you had heard on the radio that these young men had gotten a permit to go camping?" she said.

"Yes."

"So on the very first night, you were aware that they were out there camping?"

"Yes."

"And then you saw their car on the eighth?"

"Yes."

"So when you saw them on the eighth, right away you knew that they had probably been out there for four days?"

"Right."

"And at that point, the first thing that you did was go back to the visitor center and have lunch?"

"Yes."

"So you didn't sense any urgency in trying to go find them?"

"Well, they were over . . . ," Keebler began to stammer. He seemed surprised suddenly to find himself on the defensive, and crossed his arms in front of his chest. "I thought to myself that they were overdue and that's the reason I looked up Lance after I finished lunch. . . ."

"Okay. But you waited until after lunch to find Lance?"

"Yes."

Boyne owned him after that. She led him into admitting that he had no training in rescue work, that the spot where they found Kodikian—exposed on the rocks of the canyon floor—suggested he wasn't in his right mind, and that he had no knowledge whatsoever about dehydration. When Boyne was finished, Williams didn't bother to redirect.

————

Near midmorning, a compressor in the building's air conditioner blew out, allowing condensation to collect steadily in the court-house. It was almost imperceptible at first, a milkiness in the fluorescent courtroom light so faint that no one remarked. People thought it was their own fatigue, or dry contact lenses, until the bailiff whispered in Judge Forbes's ear and he apologetically explained the situation. Everyone laughed nervously, grateful that the fog hadn't come from their own failing senses.

Mark Maciha took the stand next. As the park service's most vocal critic of Kodikian's story, everyone expected his testimony to be forceful and direct. He briskly described getting called into the canyon, arriving on the scene, and treating Kodikian. When Williams quizzed him about the cairns along the trail, he talked about their placement and visibility in no uncertain terms. To him, they were facts on the ground, there for all to see, and his characterization of the conversation he had had with Kodikian was equally solid.

"Everything that I talked to him about he responded appropriately. There was no perceptible delay in responses," he said.

Mitchell began his cross-examination of the ranger in the same, casual tone he had used with Mattson.

"Now, you've been doing this for a lot of years," he said, referring to Maciha's experience as a ranger.

"Yes."

"And I suspect before you ever worked for the park service that you were an outdoorsman."

"Yes."

"And the truth of the matter is that on more than one occasion, when you were in Rattlesnake Canyon trying to find that exit, or the trail up and out of there, that you've missed that particular entrance."

"No."

Mitchell was referring to the *Philadelphia Magazine* story by Bill Gifford, who had written that Maciha himself at first hadn't been able to find the cairn marking the trail out, and quoted the ranger as saying, "I always miss that." But Maciha said he had no recollection of making the comment. "That doesn't sound like me," he said.

They went back and forth like that for twenty minutes. The ranger "couldn't say" whether or not Kodikian had made an effort to get out of the sun, and had "no idea" what the temperature inside the tent was. He disagreed with the lawyer's assessment that it was difficult to climb out of the canyon. "You just need to watch your footing," he said. It was during his cross-examination of Maciha that Mitchell first mentioned the two fire pits.

"Assuming that the boys were complying with the rules of the park, the one assumption that could be made from the lighting of the two fires was that they were trying to attract somebody's attention," Mitchell said.

"I can't make that assumption," Maciha replied.

"Well, that's one way you can attract attention in a national park, is with a fire."

"That's true," the ranger said. He sounded bored.

"I mean, we know that well today in New Mexico just because we have two raging forest fires out of control," he said, referring to the Cerro Grande blaze, and a smaller one that had flared up near Ruidoso.

Judge Forbes called a recess after Mitchell was through with Maciha, and Mitchell strolled out into the hall and sat down on a bench along the wall. Not long afterward, Maciha left the courtroom to head back to the park. After the ranger passed, Mitchell's eyes followed him all the way down the hall, almost wistfully, as if he were watching a coyote escape across the prairie with one of his chickens.

"There goes a hard man," he sighed.

———

After lunch, Les Williams played the hour-long videotape of the crime scene that Jim Ballard had taken on Monday, August 9. It was evidence logging, not prime time, but it held all the interest of a bad home video. Ballard identified the various items from the stand—the tent, the knife, the water bottles, the backpacks . . . it went on and on, and because of the debacle with the U.S. Customs helicopter, many of the same items appeared twice. Just when it seemed as if snores would spread throughout the courtroom, people suddenly realized that the scene had changed. They were watching the exhumation of David Coughlin's body.

There on the monitor was the cowboy grave, surrounded by the investigators, whose arms began moving in and out of the frame in an eerie ballet as they reached to remove the stones, one by one. First a pallid patch of skin appeared, then a leg, then his whole body was there, ringed almost regally by the remaining stones. Thankfully, his face remained covered by the blue plaid shirt, but anyone who had known David Coughlin in real life, or had even seen a photograph of him, could see that they were looking at a different man. His legs, once nearly worthy of a linebacker, now seemed inordinately long and sadly feminine. His torso was woefully flat. Not a trace of his stockiness remained. He was an empty husk.

Raffi watched with what appeared to be curiosity at first, but when his friend's body became visible, Mitchell turned to him and whispered in his ear. He then looked away from the TV monitor for the duration of the excavation. Later on, Mitchell said that he had told Raffi he didn't have to watch it if he didn't want to.

Lead investigator Eddie Carrasco, who had spent more hours working on the investigation than anyone, took the stand next and gave the shortest testimony out of all the key witnesses. He introduced eleven pieces of evidence, including the four knives, three water bottles, and the journal, then left. He was followed by Dennis Klein from the Albuquerque Medical Examiner's Office, and Mark Hopkins, the doctor who had treated Kodikian. Hopkins swore that Kodikian's sodium level, 174, was the highest he had ever seen.

The rest of the witnesses that day, and for much of the next, were all experts, in varying degrees, on dehydration. None of them disagreed about whether or not the friends were dehydrated, only to what extent. Robert Moon, the state's first expert, was especially persuasive. A biologist with the National Park Service, he had seventeen years of experience studying dehydration's effects on the human body, and he knew Edward Adolph's dizzying array of tables and calculations by heart. At the outset of the investigation, Williams had asked him to calculate how dehydrated the friends had actually been. Using only the journal as a guide to their activity, and temperature data from the park—and factoring in the water and Gatorade they had brought with them into the canyon—Moon had estimated their dehydration levels between 12 and 13 percent at the most, and 10 percent at the least. Since Coughlin's postmortem body weight—one of the most accurate gauges of dehydration—later indicated that he was about 13 percent dehydrated, Moon had been almost right on the money in his case with a very limited set of facts.

"There was certainly substantial potential for physical and psychological impairment," he conceded when Mitchell cross-examined him.

Mitchell's own dehydration expert, Dr. Spencer Hall, pushed far greater numbers, testifying that, based on his sodium levels, Kodikian could have been as much as 18 percent dehydrated—a number which, according to Adolph's work, meant that he was on the very edge of death when Mattson found him. In the end, the experts agreed that both men were bad off, but disagreed on how close to death Coughlin had been. Moon thought Coughlin would have lived; Hall thought there was a strong chance he would have been dead by the time the rangers arrived. Hall, with the last words, said that the friends had been right to think that they were going to die in the canyon.

But all the expert testimony, number crunching, and hair-splitting was about to become virtually irrelevant.

20

"Your Honor, I'd like to call Raffi Kodikian," Mitchell now announced.

Raffi rose from his spot at the defense table, crossed the well, and sat down in the stand. His face was expressionless and waiting.

"Good morning to you, Raffi," Mitchell said, as if for the first time that day.

"Morning."

"I think it's necessary for the court to learn some things about you, so we're going to ask some very central questions; then we'll get into the facts of this case. Would you tell the court your full name?"

"Raffi Paul Kodikian."

"And Raffi, when were you born?"

"December 26, 1973."

"And where were you born?"

"Lansdale, Pennsylvania."

Raffi seemed to relax as he answered the routine background questions, as if comforted by their familiarity. He had a rich, full voice, far more rounded in pronunciation than the New Mexicans with their soft twangs.

"All right, let's visit with more of the facts as it directly relates to this case," Mitchell said after the preliminaries. "This case involves you and David. Will you tell the court when and how you met David?"

"David and I met through my ex-girlfriend. He was dating her best friend at the time, and they were living in Amherst, Massachusetts, going to school out there. I was living in Boston. And they came into the city one night. That was the first time we met."

"How many years ago was that?"

"I would say it was about five years ago."

"What happened after that in terms of your friendship with David?"

"Well, because he was living a distance away we didn't see each other that much. But it was always something to look forward to when we did see each other. We immediately took to each other. Very similar people, very similar senses of humor. He was somebody I could spend time with and hang out with very easily."

"And did you do that as the years went by?"

"Frequently. As often as we could, yes. And once he moved into Boston we saw each other frequently."

"By frequently, how often is that?"

"At the minimum, once every two weeks, but more frequently on a weekly basis. At least we talked definitely on a weekly basis, if not less."

"Most of us have relationships in which we like somebody, either a neighbor or we knew them through business and whatever and we enjoy visiting with them, but was this relationship anything more than that?"

"Uh, yeah. We grew very close. Like I said we were very similar people. We kept each other laughing, which was a big part of our relationship. His sense of humor and mine meshed very well. We often finished each other's punch lines."

"Did you go to sporting events together?"

"Yes, Red Sox games, stuff like that, yeah."

"Did you go to movies?"

"All the time. It was one of the things we did most frequently."

"And let me ask you, you're under oath here today . . . were there ever any problems between you and David?"

"No. We never fought. I don't remember a disagreement once. It just wasn't part of our relationship. We usually saw things eye to eye, so we had no reason to disagree on any topics. We always got along very well."

"And there's been some innuendo about a mutual girlfriend or something, somebody that both of you knew. One, who are we talking about here?"

"I believe we're talking about my ex-girlfriend. It was never the case. Dave and her never dated. There were never any issues with it. When Kirsten and I broke up, she and David hung out frequently because they were friends, and I never had a problem with that. The three of us hung out on occasion after we broke up. Our friendship, the three of us, remained very close."

"As a matter of fact, is Kirsten here?"

"Yes," replied Raffi. He nodded toward the Kodikian side of the audience. In the second row, wearing a floral jumper, sat the woman who had been the source of so much speculation among the investigators and journalists. The Kodikians were infinitely grateful that she had come, her mere presence a powerful confirmation of Raffi's veracity.

As if to drive home his comfort with the idea of Raffi, Dave, and Kirsten together as a platonic threesome, Mitchell next displayed on the projector screen photographs of the three of them together. They were from New Year's Day, 1998, when the three had driven down to Philadelphia to watch the Mummers Parade. It was a classic down-home moment for Mitchell, showing his audience the family photo album.

"How long would you say that you and David palled around together, how many years?" Mitchell continued.

"Uh . . . we really got tight for the last three years."

"And close enough to both share and seek the advice and counsel of the other as to emotional problems, business problems, educational problems?"

"Sure, all that stuff, yeah," Raffi said. "If I had a problem that I couldn't go to Kirsten about, I went to Dave about it. Sometimes the problem *was* Kirsten, so Dave was the one who heard about it," he said, smiling. There were chuckles on both sides of the audience.

"I see. And how about David with you?"

"Same thing."

"And how close would you describe your relationship to David? What did he mean to you?"

Raffi was silent for a moment. When he finally spoke, he seemed burdened with memory and loss.

"Dave was a constant. . . . I knew that if I needed something he was there. I'd describe Dave as the closest thing I'd have to a brother."

———

"Let's talk about the trip to New Mexico, Raffi," Mitchell now said in a low, conciliatory voice, "Will you tell Judge Forbes when you first got this idea and how it came about, how you came to be on the road to New Mexico?"

"David was moving from the Boston area to California," Kodikian began, then led the courtroom through the opening of their misadventure—Dave's invitations for Raffi to come along, his initial reluctance, and the going-away dinner when he finally decided to ask for leave without pay. Then the trip itself: their mad dash to Philadelphia, Washington, D.C., Nashville, Memphis, New Orleans, and finally Austin, where, over beers at a local pool hall, they'd realized they were ahead of schedule and decided to take the advice of Coughlin's uncle and detour to Carlsbad.

"When you were in Austin, and you had had some alcohol to drink, how much?" asked Mitchell.

"I would guess at least five beers each," said Raffi. "Probably a little bit more because we weren't concerned about driving. I really don't remember."

"Okay. And had you had much in the way of water to drink on the trip from Austin to Carlsbad?"

"I'm sure we had something in the car. We tended to keep a

couple sodas or drinks with us, but I don't remember exactly how much we had."

"So we're talking about sodas and Coca-Colas or something like that?"

"We would have had probably a couple sodas and maybe a couple bottles—small bottles of Gatorade—smaller bottles than that one." He pointed to the empty bottle of Gatorade sitting on the evidence table.

"Now, was the car air-conditioned?"

"Yes."

"And from Austin to Carlsbad in August of 1999, do you recall if the air conditioner was on or off?"

"It was on," he said confidently.

"And we know from the journal what day you arrived at Carlsbad, but this is a big area here, so where was the first place you went and about what time did you get there?"

"We got into White's City. It was late afternoon. We stopped at a gas station to ask about camping in the area . . . ," he said, and told of how he and Dave drove up to the park's visitor center and asked Ranger Kenton Eash about getting a camping permit. "He gave us a pass to fill out and started trying to explain it," Raffi said of Eash, "but he really didn't seem to know what he doing—as if this was the first time he was doing it, that he had not filled one out before and he didn't really know how the process worked. Shuffling papers, not certain about what order things should go in and stuff like that. It was something that both Dave and I noticed. And then he actually said to us, 'You can see I don't know what I'm doing.' And at the time we were like, 'Don't worry about it. It's not a big deal.' And so we just . . . we got through that and we rushed down into the canyon, because at this point it was getting kind of late, and—"

"I wanna stop you before we got down to the canyon," Mitchell interrupted. "Did the ranger, whoever—I assume this was probably a student that was working there—"

"That's what we assumed, yeah."

"Did they explain to you certain rules of the park?"

"Yes."

"Tell the court what you remember."

"I remember him telling us about no campfires in the park. Pack out what you pack in, which means don't leave anything behind, I believe including waste. He told us the recommendation about the amount of water we should take. It was a gallon per day. He warned us about rattlesnakes in the area and . . . I believe that was about it."

"Did you get anything else other than the permit?"

"I asked him where we could get water. I hadn't planned on doing any serious backpacking, so I didn't bring all the supplies that I would have brought on the trip that I made across the country in ninety-seven. So I didn't have a canteen or anything like that. So we didn't have any containers, really, to put water into. He told me that the cafeteria sold water, and I went in and the one-pint bottles down there are what they sold." Raffi gestured toward the empty water bottles that Eddie Carrasco had introduced during his testimony.

"And how many did you buy?"

"I believe I bought three."

"The three that are here in court?"

"Yes, sir."

"And what else did you have in the way of liquid sustenance?"

"We had two bottles of Gatorade. I believe they were thirty-two-ounce bottles, but I'm not sure. It was that one," he said, pointing again toward the evidence table, "and an identical bottle."

"All right. So while we're on the water situation, what we have here in the courtroom—one bottle of Gatorade, three bottles of water—was that all you had?"

"We had a second bottle of Gatorade, but we left it in the car because we didn't want to have to carry it down in there. And we were just leaving it for when we got back. Our thought at the time was that we were just spending the night there. We weren't planning on spending an entire day, we weren't planning on touring the canyon. So we took less water than we needed."

"Oh, one other thing," Mitchell said. "Did you guys ever purchase a topo map?"

"Yes, we did. It suggested it in the literature that we had gotten at the visitor center, so I went into the bookstore and purchased one."

"Do you know what happened to it?"

"I believe we actually burned it with some of the other stuff. We . . . by the middle of the week we were pretty much burning about anything that would burn."

"So the map we have here in the courtroom may or may not be your map?"

"I don't think it was. It's a possibility, but I don't think so."

"All right. What time did you get to the parking spot, as best you recall, Raffi, where you guys go off down into Rattlesnake Canyon?"

"My best guess would be about six o'clock, maybe closer to seven."

"All right, now I've got you up there, you guys take off. Raffi, I have a question for you: Did you ever stop at the top and take a good look all the way around you to orient yourself as to where you were?"

"We looked at the canyon on the way in. We were looking at what was in front of us. I'd say our first mistake—in hindsight—our first big mistake as far as getting lost went was when we got to the bottom of the entrance trail we didn't turn around and look back at what we had just come down out of. We were looking ahead. We stopped for a couple of minutes and had some water, but we didn't really look around to check out our surroundings."

"By the time you got to the bottom of Rattlesnake Canyon, how much water did you have left?"

"I would guess we each had about a half bottle left. Half a pint for drinking. The third bottle we ended up using for cooking. We didn't think about that when we went down, that we would need water for dinner. So we used that bottle for cooking and then we had the thirty-two-ounce bottle of Gatorade."

"What happened to the Gatorade that night?"

"The Gatorade we drank that night."

"And what happened to the water, the rest of the water that you had?"

"The one pint was used for dinner. The other two half pints were saved for the next morning for the hike out."

"So you really have one pint of water left for the next morning?"

"When we woke up the next morning we had a pint of water left, yeah."

"When were you out of water, Raffi?"

"We finished off that water when we got to what we thought was the exit trail."

"What, in your mind, is the exit trail?"

"Well, it was the trail out of . . . The trail that we had hiked down into the canyon dumped out into a riverbed. We found a cairn and it looked familiar, and we saw a path going into the brush, so we presumed that that was the trailhead and we finished off our water there because we knew we had some more up at the car."

"So, again: You're at that point, do you drink the rest of your water?"

"Yes."

"About what time of day was that?"

"I would say it was about eight or nine in the morning."

"So at about eight or nine o'clock Thursday morning, the sixth of August, you're out of water. Is that a fair statement?"

"Yes."

―――――

"Just start telling the court what happened without my interruption," Mitchell continued, and so Raffi took a deep breath and told the story of that first, lost day; how they had searched fruitlessly for the exit trail, sought shade, and ended up kneeling on the canyon floor and sucking rainwater from between the rocks and spitting it into their empty bottles.

"At the time I was unaware that you can't ration water," he said. "I've learned that, since." He told of how they had found the cactus fruit, which became their only source of water and food for the next three days, and provided a long-awaited explanation to

Chunky Click's favorite question: Why hadn't they cracked the can of beans? "We presumed they were salted," he explained, "and we knew that it was probably more of a gravy than water. So we really weren't thinking about that, especially since we had the fruit."

He told of how, as early as that night, they speculated about how long it would take before the rangers came looking for them. "We began right away questioning the way that the permit was taken," he said, "whether or not the person that took it really knew where it was supposed to go and how it was supposed to be handled." It was that same night that they saw the mysterious headlights that inspired the laborious climb out of the canyon the next morning.

"In hindsight, the only explanation I have is that we saw a plane, and we thought it was some kind of a park service truck that was doing a route," he said of the lights, and described how the next morning they had left their tent and made the arduous hike up the canyon slopes.

"The tent was down on the canyon floor?" Judge Forbes interrupted. He, and everyone else in the courtroom, had been so still and quiet up to this point that it was easy to forget he was there, even though he was sitting right next to Raffi.

"The tent was down in the canyon floor," Raffi affirmed.

"Could you see it?"

"We could when we were out on the edge of that mountain, at the tip," Raffi replied, "but as we walked in we lost sight of the tent."

Those would be the only two questions Judge Forbes would ask Raffi, who went on to describe their decision to remain up the plateau instead of continuing on to the plains below, where Dave thought they might find a road. "There was no way that I was gonna be able to move, so I told him that if he felt he could get to it then he should go and send back help. He didn't want to leave me behind and he didn't want to go by himself," he said, and briskly described their long afternoon in the plateau's sweltering heat; the lack of shade, the biting ants, the exhaustion. When he spoke again, his voice was slow and heavy.

"Friday was when we first noticed the birds," he said, as if he could see the buzzards circling in his memory. "They were probably about thirty feet above us. It would start with just one circling and then another one would come and then another one. And they would just stick around and watch us. We would wave our arms to let them know that we were still alive. And they'd disappear, and they would come back about an hour later.

"That was the first time that Dave and I had discussed suicide. My understanding of buzzards at the time was that they start before you're done. That they'll start attacking you as soon as you're too tired to fight them. And the topic of ending it early came up. But that was it. It was just mentioned once and then we forgot about it for the time being."

Raffi resumed his steady recounting of Friday, August 6; their attempt to drink urine on the way back to their tent; how they'd mistakenly thought the rangers had come and left water on the ranch foundation; and how Dave struggled the last few hundred yards back to the tent. It was then that they had seen what they thought was a new cairn.

"The first thing we both thought was that the rangers had come down and put that cairn up basically to cover their ass," he told the courtroom, "so that nobody would say later the trail wasn't marked well enough." He recounted how they resolved to try to pick up the cairn trail the next morning, then his disturbing vision of people in the canyon building machines to make their escape. "Me and Dave didn't have what we needed to build the machines," he said, "so we were gonna be stuck."

He moved on to the following morning: their last, fruitless attempt to find the trail, the stone "SOS," and the signal fire. "We started tossing everything we had that could burn into that fire, including my sleeping bag," he said. "We threw mine as opposed to his because it was older and it was smaller and we just needed one for the night."

So far, much of Raffi's testimony about the ordeal in Rattlesnake Canyon had been consistent, in greater detail, with lines either he or Dave had written in the journal: "We will not let the buzzards get us alive. . . . Yesterday we never found the road but reached what seemed to be the furthest reaches of the park. . . . Nobody has come . . . returned to camp and built fire." But by Saturday, their journal entries had mostly been either recollections of what they had already gone through, or good-bye notes to their family and friends—not what they were going through at the time. Consequently, the whole downward spiral that led up to the killing would be based almost entirely on Kodikian's next words.

.   "And Saturday . . . Saturday was rough," he said, slowing down again. "Saturday was long and mentally painful. I've never been so aware of every second that goes by. You didn't have the distractions that you normally have in the day that speed things up. We just lied there. I remember several times looking at my watch and

thinking that an hour had gone by but it had been five or ten minutes. And mentally that was very taxing. Again, like going up the
mountain that the end wasn't in sight. It was Saturday that we cut
the bottom out of the tent. The reason we did that was because
the fly was open in front and in back and you could get a better
breeze under the tent with just the fly than you could with the
tent itself. So we dropped the tent part of it and we cut that out.
And then we . . . A little while later we noticed that the rocks
underneath the tent were cooler than the nylon or the plastic that
we were lying on, so we cut the bottom of the tent out and just
kept the outside of the tent to hold up the fly. And all day
Saturday we moved rocks back and forth to get to the cooler rocks
underneath. I remember we took small handfuls of pebbles and ran
them down our back 'cause it felt like water. And that's pretty
much the way we spent Saturday. We had stopped eating the fruit.
We weren't at all hungry and it was almost like the water we were
getting out of it was too thick with sugar, so we just stopped eating
it, we had no desire to eat it.

"I remember that there was no cloud cover at all on Saturday.
The sun was up the whole time and I remember thinking about
the sun as like a guard, and his job was to beat us into submission
and we just had to take it. Every once in a while a cloud would
come and block the sun, and it was like someone was distracting it
and we could breathe for a minute. And then it would disappear
and the sun would be back and it would be right back to the whole
thing over again.

"The sun went behind a cloud late Saturday afternoon. The
birds had been there the whole time. They had been circling
around us all day, over us all day. We crawled out from under the

tent and the sun stayed behind the cloud until night. And mentally and physically I was destroyed. I didn't know if I could go through another day like we had just gone through. It was probably about an hour later that Dave started getting sick.

"He started vomiting and nothing was coming up. In the beginning, nothing was coming up—eventually mucus started coming out, bile. But it wouldn't. . . . His voice all day Saturday had been getting progressively worse. I suspected . . . I could hear the mucus in his throat was staying there and his voice was sounding garbled. So it was difficult to understand what he was saying. When he started throwing up I figured that's what was coming up, but he couldn't get it out of his throat. He was throwing up and it would hang out of his throat and just stay there. He couldn't get it to come out all the way. So I had to help him pull it out, pull it out of his throat because it wasn't going to come out any other way. So I had to give him a hand and then pull it out of his throat for him. He was throwing up for a while, probably an hour. Sometimes it would be constant and then he would get a break and then he would start throwing up again.

"Eventually he started yelling for a doctor and saying he needed to go to a hospital. And I didn't have the heart to tell him that nobody was listening. So I started yelling with him. And then he stopped yelling and he looked at me and he said, 'I just realized.' And I said, 'What?' And he said, 'This is it.' And I think I said, 'Yeah.' He said, 'They're not coming.' And I said, 'No.'

"After sitting there all day on Saturday and nobody showing up and we were over two days late, we had no hope that they even knew were down there. We had figured that the kid who had taken the permit had put it in the wrong file or it was in the trash or it was gone, that they didn't even know we were in the canyon. And we had absolutely no hope of getting out of there. We figured that some hiker was gonna find our bodies. And Dave turned to me and he said, 'Let's do this.' And I knew what he was talking about and we talked about how we were gonna end our lives.

"We decided that since I was stronger that he would cut my wrist first and then I would cut his. I don't think that either one of us really had the strength to do it to ourselves. So I sat next to him and we got a knife and he tried cutting my left wrist. Either the knife we were using was too dull, or he wasn't pushing as hard as he should have been. But it wouldn't break through the skin all the way. We cut across my wrist, went down it. We tried each of the knives we had and none of them worked. I knew if I made any sound it was gonna be that much harder for him so I didn't make any. But I think he knew that it hurt and I really don't think he pushed as hard as he could have. We eventually gave up, we stopped, and we were both beside ourselves. We didn't know what we were gonna do, how we were gonna handle it. I bandaged up my arm. I don't really think I was worried about it getting infected, I just didn't want to look at it. And we actually tried it again, but it didn't work. He put down the knife and we pretty much decided that we were gonna have to go through whatever we were gonna have to go through, that we weren't gonna end it early. We abandoned the idea of committing suicide. They tell me that Dave had slashes on his wrist. I don't remember trying to cut his. What I remember was deciding that if it didn't work on me it wouldn't work on him so we didn't bother. There's a possibility we did but I just don't recall it.

"Dave started throwing up again. He spent the whole night on his hands and knees, throwing up. I was awake most of the time and I eventually started throwing up too. It wasn't as bad as Dave, but it happened maybe a half-dozen times for me. I don't know how many times Dave threw up. He was on his hands and knees the whole night, and when he did stop it wasn't for long. He couldn't sit down. He tried to sit down, he tried to straighten his legs out sometime early in the morning and he couldn't. His body was frozen. We eventually got him to the point where he could sit upright and he was trying to lay down because he was exhausted. And every time he tried to lay down a little bit he started getting sick. We tried it with him sitting in front of me and me sitting behind him and I would take his arms like this and he would lean back and I'd try to ease him down, but every time we'd gotten a couple inches he'd start throwing up again. And then he'd come back and we'd do it again and he'd get a bit further and get sick again. We tried that countless times, I don't know how many times we tried that.

"Eventually he got down on his back, and as soon as he did he turned to me and said, 'You've got to end this.' And at first I wasn't really sure what he meant and he said, 'Get the knife.' And I said, 'No.' I said I wasn't gonna do that. And he reached up and he grabbed me right there and he squeezed me hard, real hard, and he said, 'Stop fuckin' around.' He said, 'You know they're not coming.' And I said, 'Yeah, I know they're not coming.' And he said, 'So then get the fucking knife.' So I did, and he said, 'Put it through my chest.' I was bawling. He said, 'Get next to me and put it through my chest.' He said, 'Don't fuck up.' I got next to him and I pushed it through his chest. But I fucked up and I hit his lung, because when I pulled the knife out, air came out. I told him I had to do it again. And he said, 'Okay.' And this time I thought I hit his heart. Blood came out and he said, 'Pull it out.' I did. I asked him if he was still in pain and he said no, that he felt a lot better, and he smiled.

"I held his hand the whole time. He started getting weak and I covered his face with a T-shirt. And then he died."

21

Les Williams began his cross-examination with a question that, to this day, has no definite answer.

"You think the map that the rangers found is not the one that you had, is that correct?" he asked.

"I don't think it's the one we had, no. You're talking about the topographical map?"

"Right."

"I don't think so."

"And you think that you had that map up until the fires?"

"I believe so. I don't remember which day we burned it, but I do believe we threw it in the fire."

"So I take it the map wasn't a help to you in finding your way out?"

"I had never used a topographical map before. I had seen them. I knew what they were approximately, but I had never actually used one. We tried to make sense of where we were in relation to that map, but we couldn't. I don't know how much experience Dave's had with it. He seemed to know a little bit more about it than I did, but we couldn't justify the mountains and the hills that were around us with where we thought we were. And then we saw that the foundation wasn't where the map said it was, that made us question the entire map we had and whether or not it was accurate. We stopped even trying with the map eventually and just threw it in the fire."

"So the map was . . . You did have the map when you found the foundation, when you went up on the hill and came back down?"

"I don't remember. I remember that we had looked at the map and that we had . . . I think we had walked by the foundation when we had the map. We had walked by the foundation when we were going up the mountain on Friday, so we knew that it was there. So I don't know if we had the map Friday afternoon or not. We may have already burned it, but we were aware that the map showed a foundation. I think that map did. . . . We had two of them. One was like a copy that the park hands out with the rules and the other was the topographical map. I believe the topographical mentioned the foundation but I'm not positive."

"The first camp that you went to . . . You mentioned that you were in a hurry to get out there and get camped because you got there at about six o'clock in the afternoon?"

"No, we left about six o'clock in the afternoon, left the visitor center. We got into that camp I'd say somewhere around eight or eight-thirty. And at that point the sun had left the canyon floor, and it was starting to get dark."

"Now that camp was quite a ways from where you enter Rattlesnake Canyon, right?"

"Yes."

"About two, two and a half miles?"

"Okay."

"If you were just gonna stay the night, why did you go so far back to find a place to camp?"

"Because we thought that there was actually a camping area. We didn't realize that you were just supposed to camp along the trail someplace. It said, 'Don't camp on the canyon floor.' So every time we went around a corner or went around a turn—because it runs like that, it's an 'S' through the mountains—we figured that the campsite was just around the corner. We would get around the corner and it wasn't there so we tried one more. And we did that probably two or three S's until we just said we gotta camp here. I don't even know if there is a campsite or an area that's designated for camping, but at that point we realized that it was just too far away and we were gonna camp where we were."

"Now you say that when David asked you to kill him, your first answer was no."

"Yes."

"So you knew what he was asking you to do at that time, right?"

"Yeah."

"You knew that he wanted you to kill him and he was going to be dead and he was never going to recover?"

"*I* was going to be dead," Kodikian said brusquely.

"He was going to be dead when you killed him?"

"He was going to be dead, and I was going to be dead shortly after, yes."

"So you knew what you were doing?"

"In the sense that I remember it, and that then I knew what he needed, yeah. I recognized the situation, yeah."

"So I take it that when you said that you thought you were both going to be dead that you didn't think it would matter, since both of you were going to be dead?"

"What I thought I was doing was keeping my friend from going through twelve to twenty-four hours of hell before he died," Kodikian said with an undeniably self-righteous edge. "That's what I thought I was doing."

"But I mean, you knew that you were killing him?"

"Yes, yes sir."

"You didn't think that you were killing the devil or anything like that?"

"No."

"And since you said no the first time, you could have resisted. In other words, you could have decided *not* to kill him, couldn't you?"

"I could have made that decision, yes. I could have crawled out from under the tent and gotten away from him and just listened to his pain from a distance, yeah. I could have done that."

"And it seems that you do suffer from remorse, that you're sorry you did this, because you realize that if you hadn't killed him, he'd still be alive, don't you?"

"For about the last nine months, for about the last eight months, I've felt that way, yeah. It has not been until recently that whether or not Dave would have survived has been called into question. I don't know now that he would have survived that, and to a certain extent if I found out that he wouldn't have it would make me feel a little better, knowing that he wouldn't have made it and that I did the right thing, I made the right decision. I don't know now that he would have walked out of that canyon alive. And if he had there's a good chance that he wouldn't have walked out as the Dave that I know."

"Well, he certainly wouldn't have *walked* out."

"No, he wasn't gonna walk out of there."

"He would have flown out with you."

"Uh-huh."

"So it wasn't mental illness that made you kill him, it was mercy—is that what we're saying?"

"That's the way I see it, yeah."

Williams, paused, letting the admission sink in.

"I have no further questions," he said, and left the podium.

His cross-exam couldn't have lasted more than ten minutes, and many in the audience were surprised that he hadn't grilled Kodikian further. He certainly could have attempted to corner him about his haziness about the missing map, the burning of the sleeping bag, and why—with not one, but four sharp knives in their possession—their suicide pact had been only skin deep. In Williams's defense, the bottom line was that he chose to believe Kodikian based on the facts he had in front of him, and having been convinced of his remorse, knew that there was no need to be cruel. He already had a conviction the moment Kodikian agreed to a plea bargain, and from then on there was only one thing he was intent on proving: that Raffi Kodikian knew what he was doing when he killed Coughlin. He had succeeded magnificently when Kodikian admitted precisely that, despite the fact that Raffi's own lawyers had gone to great lengths to show the contrary.

Mitchell and Boyne, in fact, attempted to throw Kodikian's mental abilities into question even further with their next three witnesses, all mental health experts, who testified that Kodikian was, in fact, all but mentally handicapped when it came to his spatial and visual recognition abilities—and yet somehow, quite miraculously, wasn't aware of it. Dr. Thomas Thompson, a neuropsychologist, went as far as saying that, based on written tests Kodikian had taken a week earlier, that "a topographical map would have been impossible for him to read," and that his foray into Rattlesnake Canyon was "a disaster waiting to happen."

None of them, however, were able to account for why Coughlin had apparently been just as clueless. The closest they came was a suggestion that, because Kodikian had such strong verbal abilities (Mitchell would even call Raffi a "genius" when it came speaking and writing), he may have influenced Coughlin's decisions for the worse, overconfidently leading his friend deeper into the demon's mouth. "It was a bunch of junk," Les Williams would later say of the psychologist testimony; he had never disputed that Raffi and David had been lost to begin with, and didn't think Mitchell needed an expert to explain how people stayed lost in a national park wilderness, especially once they were out of water. In fact, Williams thought the expert testimony gave Raffi and Dave far too little credit. "They did a lot of things right," he pointed out. Following headlights, leaving notes, seeking shade during peak temperatures—all of them were logical moves, they just hadn't been enough.

Even Raffi himself was reluctant to believe some of the experts in his own corner, a few of whom he had met only a week earlier and, in their defense, had a very limited basis on which to judge him.

Dr. Thompson, for example, testified that people with strong visual and spatial abilities were typically "really good home builders, really good craftsmen who build furniture, people who can take and visualize and conceptualize and move these things around in their head," his point being that Raffi totally lacked those skills. Clearly Thompson hadn't seen the cages Raffi'd designed and built for his pet snakes, which incorporated just about every skill he supposedly didn't possess.

Whether true or not, the visual-spatial recognition theory was certainly good for a joke. Back at the Stevens Inn later that day, Raffi was hanging out with Jeff Rosen and Kevin Guckaven, who had come out to New Mexico to support their friend and provide character testimony. They were staying four doors down from him, and when Raffi told them he was heading back to his room, Rosen and Guckaven couldn't resist the open shot.

"Kev and I said, 'Raff, don't get lost. You're just gonna go down to the left, four doors. We know you have no sense of direction, right?' Rosen remembered.

Raffi went back to his room with a smile.

———

Kirsten Swan was the first to take the stand when the sentencing hearing moved on to its final phase, character testimony.

Every eye in the courtroom turned as she rose to take the stand. When Mitchell had pointed her out during Raffi's testimony, there had been much speculation among the reporters as to whether or not she'd testify, but she had sat so quietly since then that they had more or less forgotten she was there.

"Do you know Raffi, and did you know David?" Mitchell began.

"I did, very well, they were two of my closest friends in Boston," she said.

"We have a series of photographs today that we looked at during Raffi's testimony. Are you the woman that's in the photographs?"

"Yes, that's me."

"I hate to be the one to ask you this," Mitchell said, "but in all these cases there always seems to be some vicious rumor out there about things, because people have a right to be curious and they're curious about things. But I'd like to know if there were ever any problems between David and Raffi that you were aware of?"

"Never," she said forcefully. "Never in my experience, in any of the time that I spent with them together, was there ever any tension. It was always light and fun and just a good time, never."

"In particular, was there ever a fight over you?"

She laughed as if the question were completely absurd.

"Never. My relationship with Dave was completely platonic. We were the closest of friends; he was my confidant. He and I also went to the movies together. We had gone on a trip to California together, but it never went beyond that. It was a wonderful relationship, but again, strictly platonic."

"And was Raffi aware of that?"

"Yes."

"Were there ever any problems in that regard?"

"No, never. If anything, there's always been an open line of communication on all fronts. Just between Raffi and I, even after we broke up, he still remained one of my closest friends. And we did spend some time apart, so that was never an issue. It was a nonissue. There was no romantic inclination on either of our parts. I mean, Dave was more like a brother to me than a romantic interest, so that was never—that never came into question ever."

"So it was never a problem between the three of you, and how the rest of the world thought it was a problem was beyond you?"

"That's right," she said, laughing again.

Mitchell then asked her to describe Raffi's personality, both the good and the bad. "He is the best of friends to have," she said. "He is absolutely committed to his friends and family. Perhaps, in my experience of all the people that I've met, among the most committed. I'm lucky that he's in my life, and I think that there are a lot of other people that feel that way, too."

"And the bad qualities?"

"Well, having been formerly his girlfriend for three and a half years, he's certainly strong-willed. And we had our tiffs, but always communicated well. Maybe a little stubborn, never put his clothes in the hamper. But never, never violent. Even in all the fights that we had, we kind of came to a meeting of minds over time and I don't have anything really bad to say about Raffi, I don't."

"And, you know, I'd think it would be good for us all to know something about David. So what can you tell us about David?"

"Personally to me, he was a very special person in that, because he was one of my closest friends, you know. It always amazed me, the minutiae that Dave remembered about my life when I would sit down and talk to him and kind of work through things that were happening at work or relationship issues. He was absolutely there for me in the way that a friend should be. We just enjoyed one another's company, had our own private jokes. Again, one of my very close friends in Boston."

"Let me ask you this: you're friends of both, do you know— 'cause I've asked this of other witnesses—do you know of anything evil between the two of them, anything of a malicious nature between the two of them, David and Raffi?"

"Absolutely not, never. Never have I seen anything along those lines," she said, and with that Mitchell let her go.

"Mr. Williams?" the judge asked.

Les Williams had seen Terry Cunningham's police report. "Mr. Connelly informed me that on one occasion that David told him that he had been intimate with Swan," were the exact words the Wellesley police chief had used. If everything in that report was true, then either Dave had lied to Terry Connelly, or Kirsten Swan had just lied to the court. But Les had already decided not to go down that road, and what would it have proven if he had?

"I have no questions," he said.

The rest of the character testimony moved quickly after that. Jeff Rosen and Kevin Guckaven talked about what a great friend Raffi was. They used words like "integrity" and "loyalty" and "fun-loving," and no one expected them to say otherwise, but there were some moments when the need to say something honest became as important as the need to say something good. "He might be a bit stubborn sometimes," Rosen offered when Mitchell asked him if Raffi had any bad qualities. Guckaven was more diplomatic. "He likes to hold his own opinions and carry them out," he said. "He's very strong-minded as far as that goes. If he has an opinion about something, he's willing to discuss it with you and make his point." The most flattering comments came from Katherine Swan, Kirsten Swan's mother, who had flown out with her daughter to show her support: "Raffi is the kind of man I would have liked my daughter to marry," she said. "I hoped he would have been my son-in-law and one point in time, when they broke up, I was sad about it. He was, of all the men she brought home, my favorite."

When Hal Kodikian took the stand, he was full of generosity. He thanked "everybody in Carlsbad," even the sheriff, and especially the Coughlin family. "I hope I could be as gracious if I lost a son," he said. He looked directly at Raffi when he spoke. "You're stubborn at times, Raffi, you are," he told him. "And you don't listen to your old man quite a bit, I know that." Then, almost as an afterthought, he said, "It's been great to have him home."

But perhaps the words that gave people the most to think about came from Ara Asadorian, a cousin of Raffi's who had flown in from New York: "It's very painful to be here and see such a good man in such a terrible circumstance. I think the lesson and the thing to be understood here is that under the right condition and circumstances, a bad thing can happen to a good man."

The last witness to take the stand in the *State of New Mexico v. Raffi Kodikian* was Peter Bigfoot, a survival expert from Arizona. When reporters first saw his name on a list of defense witnesses a few days earlier, a few of them wondered if Mitchell was planning to be the first lawyer in history ever to call a Sasquatch to the stand.

"Who is he?" one of them had asked Gary Mitchell.

"Oh, you'll see," he said. "If he comes. I'm actually not sure where Mr. Bigfoot is, but if he does show up you're gonna love him."

On that last day of the hearing, a man who must have been at least six foot two was sitting by himself in the back of the courtroom. He wore tan corduroys and had a shaggy silver beard and a pair of smiling black eyes on a clever, feline face, and his solitary perch in the back smacked of nothing if not an outdoorsman's shyness among house cats. He had spent much of the last twenty-two years of his life alone in the deserts of the Southwest, he explained when he took the stand, testing his ability to survive, unlocking the curative secrets of its plants and herbs, and assimilating the desert's scorched lore. He'd written three books on desert herbology, and now ran the Reevis Mountain School of Self-Reliance in Arizona, where Shawn Boyne had tracked him down in the hopes that he could fill in some of the holes in Kodikian's story.

"Have you had any personal experience with dehydration?" she asked him.

"I've had a lot of personal experience with dehydration. I think the most noteworthy was back in 1976. I walked eighty-five miles across the Sonoran Desert without any food or water," he said from the stand later that afternoon, as if he were recalling a typical day at the office. "It was in the summertime and daytime temperatures were up to one hundred thirty degrees in the sun. My first day out I didn't have anything to drink for the whole day. By about noon, my mouth was so dry that it would be about as dry as my clothes are now. And by the end of the day when I finally got to the water hole that I was looking for (and I was traveling by map and compass at this time), I was in pretty serious condition for water. And the water hole that I was looking for had a decomposing dead cow in it. I drank probably about five gallons of that water. Perhaps to give you an idea how desperate people get for water, to drink next to a decomposing dead cow, but that was the only moisture around."

There were groans in the audience, but people were clearly entertained. Even Raffi seemed intrigued as he listened, and for a moment it was possible to forget that all of this was testimony in a court of law. It felt more like a campsite, with Bigfoot, the wizened elder of the range, telling stories next to the fire.

"As I'm in my normal state of being well fed and with plenty of water, I have an awareness around me—and I think most people do—of maybe a mile or so of view, just clear thought about what's around us and where we fit in it. And that kept coming in on me to where I got seriously dehydrated I sat down to rest and when I would stand up I'd just fall down and wake up on the ground. At that time dehydration was so bad that my awareness was only right here, in the suffering of my body. I couldn't think in terms of what's a mile away or more, or what's a hundred yards, or even ten feet. All I could think of was what was right here, in the suffering of my body," he said, holding his hand to his heart.

"Do you have any experience with the prickly pear cactus?" Boyne asked.

"Yes. I'll just expand on that," he said. "When I first started teaching survival skills I had read, but I didn't have firsthand experience about it, that the prickly pear cactus were edible, and in the first class that I taught, one of my students decided to eat a prickly pear pad for lunch. And about two hours later—this was a one-day class—he became very ill, and we had to carry him almost a mile back to the vehicles. And I stayed up with this guy all night long trying to keep him alive, and he was just extremely ill, all night long, and that was just from one prickly pear cactus leaf. So that was where I first became aware I needed to study more about this."

After experimenting on his own, Bigfoot concluded that the prickly pears were safe to eat only if they were thoroughly ripe, without any tartness, and described yet another occasion when a woman ignored his warnings and insisted on eating tart, unripe prickly pears. "She was convulsing and screaming from pain," he said. "She had eight quarts of water, and six sleeping bags to keep her warm, and she was still shivering. She was retching."

Although Bigfoot's testimony seemed to come as afterthought, he was the only witness to offer a possible explanation as to why Coughlin had seemingly been so much worse off than Kodikian—a bad reaction to unripe cactus fruit.

22

After Peter Bigfoot left the stand, Les Williams returned to the podium. His somber, hunched stance seemed loaded with the weight of the closing argument he was about to make.

"Your Honor, where there is life, there is hope," he said. "The defendant purposely took David Coughlin's life. I realize at the time he felt there was no hope, but obviously there was. David Coughlin would be alive today if Raffi Kodikian had not killed him. Thousands of years of experience, wisdom, and thought make up the law. And the law says you may not murder another person just because you think it's in their best interest. The practical common-sense reason for that is shown by this case. The reason we had our experts come in and compute the amount of dehydration was to show that David still would have survived. By body weight, he was approximately 11 percent to 12 percent dehydrated. He would have survived if he had not been killed. Even if, possibly, he may have died, the law still says you cannot kill him. The defendant thought it was the right thing to do, but it was not. . . .

"I think it's clear from his testimony and from other testimony that he was not demented. He knew what he was doing. He knew he was killing his best friend. He did it on purpose to save his friend from pain and agony. This does not discount that this was a dreadful situation. It was awful, both the defendant and David were in great pain, and frankly, when he said he was without hope, based on what had happened so far, that was a reasonable conclusion. Because they had not been found, obviously they were not able to walk out anymore, so it was certainly reasonable for him to think that he was going to die and it was going to be painful. But the law says you do not kill another person. And the people from the park service who had dealt with numerous people who were lost and dying from dehydration say this is the only time that one person has killed another person in these situations."

Pausing, Williams walked over to the evidence table and picked up the knife that Kodikian had used to kill Coughlin.

"As further evidence that he knew what he was doing, he said that they had a suicide pact and the only reason they didn't complete it was that the knife wasn't sharp enough. *This knife,*" he said, holding it up, "is sharp enough to cut your wrist. This knife is sharp enough to go through your chest. The real reason they didn't commit suicide was they believe, as I said, where there's life, there's hope. And even though they intellectually thought they were going to die, they didn't really want to kill themselves. When I said there's life, there's hope, the defendant thought that, too, because he did not kill himself after he killed his friend.

"It's a hard thing that you have to do, because this defendant is not an evil person. He's not a bad person. But he did do a bad thing, and he did it purposefully and he did it knowingly. Actions speak louder than words. That's why we can say he didn't really feel there was no hope because he didn't kill himself, too. Just as his actions speak louder than words, the court's actions will also. We have responsibility in the law to look beyond this case to other cases where defendants may be in similar situations and may need to know you will not be forgiven for violating the law. You will not be forgiven for killing your friend. You are not to do it, period. Situational ethics do not apply. You do not get to murder anybody. You do not get to murder your friend. You do not get to mercy kill. That's the law in the state of New Mexico and in almost every other state. This court must sentence this defendant severely, to teach people they may not place themselves above the law, whether they are a good person, whether they are a caring person, whatever. They must follow the law by not murdering."

As Judge Forbes took in the prosecutor's words, a look of hard shock set into his face, as if during all the testimony—all the theorizing, storytelling, and hairsplitting—he had forgotten that the onus of deciding punishment was his, and now it was staring him in the face. His eyes widened when Williams first mentioned the word "law," and the prosecutor picked up on it: he had said it again and again with chastening redundancy, determined that Judge Forbes remember his decision had to be based not on his heart, but on that small, unbending word.

Peter Bigfoot, who had returned to his perch in the back of the courtroom, was all heart. He was so ruffled by Williams's demand for a harsh sentence that halfway through he raised his right hand high above his head, as if to ask a question, and held it up throughout most of Williams's closing argument. The judge and everyone else ignored him, until he finally sat back down and seemed reluctantly to accept that this was not a classroom, and that no one was going to allow him to speak. Later he would explain: "I wanted to say that when you're in a situation like that—dehydrated, with low blood sugar, sunburned, heat-exhausted, shocked by being lost, in excruciating pain from cactus poisoning—no human being can think straight under those conditions," he said. "It is impossible to make rational decisions. You'd have to be superhuman. If a person has ever experienced these conditions, they should be compassionately judged."

That, of course, was exactly the gist of what Gary Mitchell said (in many more words) in his own closing argument moments later.

"There's a saying, Your Honor, that bad cases have a tendency to make bad law," he began, and went into a soft-spoken, conversational spiel that included references to the Donner party, Jack Kevorkian, and even his own uncle, who had endured the Bataan Death March.

"I agree with Mr. Williams," he said. "We don't allow mercy killings in the state of New Mexico. But this is not a mercy killing in and of itself, this is not a Kevorkian-type case in which states struggle with a physician coming in and taking somebody's life at the request of the patient. We're not dealing with that; this isn't the Rio Rancho case, in which [Kevorkian's] assistant is being prosecuted for a similar type offense. And I say it's not because this is not a situation in which, one, obviously Raffi's not a physician. It's not made with the intellectual capabilities and concentration and rationalization that physicians and patients make in those type cases. We have a young man who makes that decision based upon the love of his best friend and upon the inability to rationalize what's going on at the time. And in great pain and agony. Far removed from those types of cases.

"It is more analogous to those type of cases that we never see in courtrooms, that we never bring up, that we only learn about after decades have gone by and young men have become old men, and they tell them to their grandchildren. We only learn of these types of cases then. We only learn about them when somebody in the twilight of their years is writing a book about what they did in World War II or what they did in Vietnam. That's where we learn about these things, and those types of cases are never brought before anybody because we understand as human beings that there are those types of situations in which we do what we think is best, not because we think about the law, not because we care about the law at the time, but because we care about our fellow man. And there is something higher than law that most of us believe."

Mitchell wound up his argument by citing the fact that there had "not been a single cry from the victim's family for some type of incarceration" and that the "deep compassion" of the people of the Southwest would allow them to understand if Raffi received a light sentence. He asked Judge Forbes to take into account that there had been no evil intent behind the killing. He asked for either a suspended or deferred sentence. And finally, he asked for the same thing that David Coughlin had allegedly asked for in the predawn gloom of Rattlesnake Canyon.

"We should receive mercy from the criminal justice system," he said.

No one would have been surprised if Judge Forbes had spent a week hunkered in his chambers, reviewing the case, mulling over the angels and devils of every possible sentence. But he had made his mind up before the closing arguments had even begun. When the lawyers were through, he announced his sentence.

"Historically, sentencing has the components of rehabilitation and retribution. Crime, I think we all know, needs to be deterred. This deterrence can be of a general nature when a court's concern is to discourage the general public from violating a law as a result of observing the sentence that is imposed against a person like you, Mr. Kodikian, and this high-profile set of circumstances and facts that challenge moral and legal reasoning. Specific deterrence, on the other hand, serves to deter you individually from violating the law in the future, and I find that it's unlikely that Mr. Kodikian will find himself in the situation that we've heard about for the past two days. The improbability of a reoccurrence turns the court's thoughts along a path of a consideration more of a general deterrence. A long period of incarceration, what the state has asked for—a severe sentence (and both attorneys have different views as to what punishment should be meted in this situation) . . . but long incarceration I think has been proved here to not be the solution. I believe that it's predictable that Raffi does not pose a threat or danger to society.

"I do, however, think that Raffi Kodikian deserves to be punished for his violation of the law and the taking of the life of his friend, David Coughlin. Retribution in this court's mind serves the very important and crucial purpose of preserving the rule of law that we all have to have for an orderly society. . . . Raffi Kodikian's conduct in this situation caused the life of David Coughlin to end.

Mr. Coughlin was a particularly vulnerable victim, and the impact on his family is never and will never be forgotten by them. I do know that Raffi's conduct was not a result of a sustained criminal intent. His character and attributes that I have heard and read about suggest that he's not likely to reoffend. His mental condition, I do believe, contributed to his conduct, but I find that he had a conscious and rational understanding of what he did at the time that he murdered David Coughlin. Raffi's remorse is genuine, I don't question that.

"It is the court's sentence that Raffi be sentenced to fifteen years in the corrections department of the state of New Mexico, and the execution of that sentence be suspended with the exception of twenty-four months."

His gavel fell lightly to the block.

———

Raffi Kodikian accepted his sentence, but not without tears. He raised his hands to his face to hide them, but there are no private gestures in a courtroom. Some people said they were the sincere sobs of a man who truly regretted his act and feared what lay ahead; others wondered if they were tears of gratitude at having received such a light sentence. Perhaps they were both.

Raffi's family and friends appeared, for the most part, relieved. The first three rows of the left side of the courtroom became a wave of hugs and lowering heads, sighs and groans, as if they were shaking off all the emotional exhaustion of the last nine months. Even though they had hoped beyond hope that he wouldn't end up in prison, they knew it could have gone much worse.

Reactions in the rest of the courtroom were torn. None were as starkly different or unexpected as those of two women, Sharene Brown, the court reporter, and Jane Smith, the bailiff. Brown spoke in a soft and chirpy voice filled with the hospitality of the Southwest. She came to court every day well made up and often in a dress, and was a picture of feminine warmth. "I couldn't believe that's all he got," she said. "I thought he was lying through his teeth. I wasn't emotional during his testimony, I was skeptical." Smith, on the other hand, the court cop who called "all rise" in a deep, commanding voice and had even jokingly proclaimed herself a "cast-iron bitch" began crying uncontrollably after Forbes passed his sentence. "We're not supposed to show any emotion," she later said, "but it was really hard to keep it together. He shouldn't have done it, but I sure didn't want him to get prison time. I don't think he should be punished at all." It had been Raffi's testimony, she explained, that had caused her iron to rust.

A few minutes later, Kodikian, Mitchell, and Boyne walked upstairs to the courthouse's third floor, where they held a short press conference. "I still feel I did the right thing," Raffi told the reporters. "I feel that anybody in my position who would turn their back on their friend in that position wouldn't be deserving of coming out of that canyon in the first place."

"How do you feel about the sentence?" one reporter asked him.

"This is a life sentence," he said. "I will spend the rest of my life trying to justify my actions."

Gary Mitchell initially told the reporters he didn't know whether or not they'd appeal the two-year sentence—a right Raffi had reserved under the plea agreement—but it was clear he had said it more out of sympathy for his client than out of any intention to do so. The appeals process, he knew, could very well take longer than the sentence itself. Later on, away from the reporters, he was clearly elated. "This was a fair sentence," he said. "I was expecting about five years. Raffi was fortunate in many ways. He was fortunate to get this judge, and he was fortunate to get this prosecutor, a man more interested in seeing justice done than in nailing heads to the wall. He was fortunate to get out of that canyon alive."

Many attributed Kodikian's light sentence more to Les Williams's restraint than to Gary Mitchell's sermons of the range. It wasn't hard to imagine a younger, hell-bent prosecutor ratcheting up Kodikian's sentence a month here and a year there by gratuitously dissecting some of his testimony. It could have been easily done. Williams could have asked Kodikian if he and Coughlin had seen the water towers from the top of the canyon. Had the answer been no, he could have shown how they were almost impossible *not* to see. He could have asked Kodikian how it was he had remembered, in great detail, the conversation he'd had with Kenton Eash, the climb up the slopes, and his dream about the machines, and at the same time been uncertain as to whether he'd burned the topo map or lost it. He could have asked Kodikian if he knew how Coughlin ended up with a three-inch bruise at the base of his skull.

But Williams had no evidence to prove that Kodikian had acted in rage, and Kodikian certainly wasn't going to offer any, so he had stuck to the truth he knew and proven what he had set out to prove from the beginning: Kodikian had admitted he knew what he was doing.

"I didn't know what to expect," Williams said of the sentence. "Before we started the hearing, I thought about eight years would be right. After we finished it, the two is fine, because we found out more. His remorse looked pretty real to me."

Only Raffi Kodikian can say for sure what happened in the early hours of August 8, 1999, and whether or not he told the truth—and many believe he did—it is disputable that he got away with anything. Just before five P.M., his friends and family escorted him to the Eddy County Jail, and the following morning he was shackled, put on a corrections department bus, and taken to the Central New Mexico Correctional Facility to be processed. From there, he got on another bus and headed east, bound for a lockup near the town of Santa Rosa, where he would serve out his sentence. It was a trip of about four hundred miles in all, and it is safe to say that it was the loneliest one of his life. For the last hundred or so miles, the bus sped east along I 40, and right next to it, visible through the barred windows, was the older road the interstate had replaced. It was the cement fable itself, Route 66.

EPILOGUE

Carlsbad returned to normal after the hearing. The TV trucks and reporters raced north to cover the fire, and the motels along Canal Street once again sat mostly empty. That is not to say that things got boring, because, unlike the water, strange news never evaporates on that scratch of the map. Later that summer, a swarm of killer bees attacked an elderly woman in town, causing her to die of a heart attack in her own garden. That sad event was followed by an even sadder one, weeks later, when a section of natural gas pipeline along the Pecos exploded, shooting a stream of flames two hundred yards, right to a spot where ten people, including five children, were camping. All ten of them died. But the strangest story of all happened the following spring.

Almost a year after Kodikian's sentencing hearing, Brian Tenney, a thirty-five-year-old Pennsylvanian, was hiking through Rattlesnake Canyon when he noticed an envelope lying on the canyon floor. Inside was a letter written two days earlier by a woman named Emily Schulman. She explained that she was lost in Rattlesnake Canyon and needed help. In case it never came, she had also written her good-byes to her friends and family. The return address on the envelope was in Boston, Massachusetts.

Being from Pennsylvania, Tenney had heard all about the Kodikian case, and he knew he was walking over the same ground. "I thought it was a hoax someone pulled," Tenney later told the *Carlsbad Current-Argus*. "I figured some college kid was watching me with binoculars laughing."

His skepticism toward the note quickly turned to concern, however, when he came across torn-up bits of paper nearby. They were pieces of ripped-up business cards, with more notes from Schulman asking for help. He ran much of the way back out of the canyon, then raced back to the visitor center in his car.

Within minutes teams of rangers and law enforcement officers were winding down the Rattlesnake Canyon trail. Many of the same players were there, including Mark Maciha and Jim Ballard, both of whom noticed that Schulman's car was parked in the exact spot where Coughlin's Mazda had been. And after they hiked down into the canyon, their search for Schulman took them right past the spot where Lance Mattson had found Kodikian, lying next to the body of his friend.

They searched for hours in vain, until the sheriff's office finally called in a search plane. But this story had a happy ending: the plane spotted Schulman shortly after three P.M. She was about a mile west of the exit trail, waving a T-shirt with all her might. When her rescuers finally reached her, she was almost out of water. She told them that she had come to the canyon two days earlier for a day hike, and missed the exit trail.

"It was weird," Maciha later said over the phone. "I don't know what to make of it. I really don't know what we can do to make that trail any more visible."

It was a bitter vindication for the families of both David and Raffi, who had always been of the opinion that Raffi never would have been driven to mercy killing if the trail had been better marked and rangers had noticed that they were overdue earlier. After the sentencing hearing, the Coughlins had even set up a fund to equip the park with GPS systems that hikers in the back-country could check out at the visitor center, but Schulman was either unaware of it, or more likely never bothered checking in at the main desk.

After the *State of New Mexico v. Raffi Kodikian*, most of the law enforcement and legal professionals involved continued working on less-ambiguous cases, with just as much zeal. Gary McCandless and Eddie Carrasco went back mainly to busting drug dealers, and Les Williams happily returned to prosecuting them. Gary Mitchell continues to fight against the death penalty with great success. Shawn Boyne eventually got tired of the long hours, and she took a professorship at a university. Her involuntary intoxication defense made Law Review.

Chunky Click lost his reelection bid in November, then took a job in the police department in the nearby town of Loving. To this day, he still believes that Raffi Kodikian got away with murder.

According to prison officials, Kodikian was a model inmate. His good behavior, and changes in New Mexico state law giving corrections authorities more discretion over prison terms, reduced his time served to sixteen months. He was released in November 2001, and made it home for Thanksgiving.

David Coughlin will never make it home, but at least a part of him made it to what would have been his next stop on the road to California. "Dave has asked that his remains be cremated & thrown over the edge of the Grand Canyon," Raffi had written in the journal, and his family took the words to heart. In August 2001, two years after he died in Rattlesnake Canyon, the Coughlins made the trek out to Arizona and scattered his ashes into the greatest canyon of all.

ACKNOWLEDGMENTS

This book would have been far more difficult to produce if it weren't for the assistance of many people. I thank them here, beginning with everyone who was willing to be interviewed, at times in spite of their reluctance. Journalism of the dead is an inherently difficult task, often involving asking people to access emotions and memories they'd rather not relive or make public. I am particularly grateful to those people who decided to share their memories of David Coughlin. They are the only voice he has left.

I'd also like to thank my fellow journalists, some of whom covered the Rattlesnake Canyon case themselves for their respective media outlets and freely offered their insights, help, and encouragement. They are: Kyle Marksteiner and Jose Martinez, Jim Kaminsky, Todd Katz, Jay Cheshes, Sheri de Borchgrave, Laurina Gibbs, Loch Adamson, Tanya Henderson, Sally Hawkins, Connie Chung, Scott MacBlane, Steph Watson, Alistair Bates, and Philip Jones Griffiths, for his wonderful photos and insight.

Then there are the information providers: all the wonderful folks at the Eddy County Courthouse, Sally Bickley, Sherry Fletcher, the *Northeastern News*, and Garmin International, for use of their GPS and topo maps, and anyone I'm forgetting.

Last but not least, my parents and Scott Waxman, Dan Conaway, and Nikola Scott. Their patience was a godsend.